Hosea

Love When It Matters Most

Hosea

Love When It Matters Most

By
Dr. Bo Wagner

Word of His Mouth Publishers
Mooresboro, NC

All Scripture quotations are taken from the **King James Version** of the Bible.

ISBN: 978-1-941039-54-0
Printed in the United States of America
©2025 Dr. Bo Wagner

Word of His Mouth Publishers
Mooresboro, NC
www.wordofhismouth.com

All rights reserved. No part of this publication may be reproduced in any form without the prior written permission of the publisher except for quotations in printed reviews.

Table of Contents

	Introduction... 7	
1	The Least Likely of Love Stories................................. 9	
2	The Glow and the Gathering Darkness......................... 19	
3	Broken Home, Broken Heart 35	
4	A Door of Hope... 53	
5	Love When It Matters Most....................................... 67	
6	I Have a Bone to Pick With You 83	
7	Idolatry/Adultery, Adultery/Idolatry 97	
8	When God Cannot Be Found 109	
9	Coming Back to God—But Will It Matter................... 123	
10	Of Kings and Bakers... 131	
11	Sowing the Wind and Reaping the Whirlwind 143	
12	Wanderers Among the Nations 153	
13	The Dangers of a Divided Heart 171	
14	The Turning of the Tide 185	
15	Shadows of the Past, Stains of the Present 197	
16	The Quickest Path to Struggleville 209	
17	I Will Love Them Freely.. 223	
	Works Cited 235	
	Other Books by Dr. Bo Wagner 237	

Introduction

Love stories abound in our world. But if it is to be a contest on which true human love story is the best, the deepest, the most profound, the most overcoming, then the contest will quickly be over.

Hosea will win, and it will not even be particularly close.

Mind you, other love stories are certainly of note; the Song of Solomon comes to mind. But no other true human love story takes you from a breathless, unbelievably unlikely start, to the height of bliss, then to the depths of betrayal, then to the agony of brokenness, ending with reconciliation that no one could ever have seen coming, least of all the one who had done the betraying.

And all of it, though absolutely historical and true, is also the most amazing picture of the love of God for His people that could ever be imagined by the combined power of all of the most creative minds in existence.

There is simply nothing quite like it.

Hosea really is *Love When It Matters Most.*

Chapter One
The Least Likely of Love Stories

Hosea 1:1 *The word of the LORD that came unto Hosea, the son of Beeri, in the days of Uzziah, Jotham, Ahaz, and Hezekiah, kings of Judah, and in the days of Jeroboam the son of Joash, king of Israel.* **2** *The beginning of the word of the LORD by Hosea. And the LORD said to Hosea, Go, take unto thee a wife of whoredoms and children of whoredoms: for the land hath committed great whoredom, departing from the LORD.* **3** *So he went and took Gomer the daughter of Diblaim; which conceived, and bare him a son.*

A backdrop of prosperity

Hosea 1:1 *The word of the LORD that came unto Hosea, the son of Beeri, in the days of Uzziah, Jotham, Ahaz, and Hezekiah, kings of Judah, and in the days of Jeroboam the son of Joash, king of Israel.*

As we begin to examine the Minor Prophets, Hosea to Malachi, it would be good for us to know a bit about them as a whole.

Let's begin with where they fit in the timeline of Israel. The twelve minor prophets ministered from approximately 823 B.C. to 400 B.C., with Jonah being the first chronologically and Malachi being the last. So they ministered roughly from the time of Jeroboam II up through the fall of Judah to Babylon and then went on until the three major returns from exile had taken place, the wall and Temple were rebuilt, and the Silent Years began. Put in terms of the historical books of the Bible, if you opened your Bible and put your index finger in 2 Kings 14, that is roughly where the ministry of the Minor Prophets began, and if you then flipped ahead to the book of Esther and put your thumb there, the minor prophets mostly ministered in the time period of those pages you would be holding between your index finger and thumb.

The Minor Prophets are called the Minor Prophets simply because they are not as long as the writings of three of the Major Prophets, Isaiah, Jeremiah, and Ezekiel, or quite as far-reaching in their influence as Daniel. They are every bit as inspired, though, and every bit as important.

They are also, surprising to many, incredibly relevant for us today.

As to our first Minor Prophet, Hosea, we learn in verse one that he ministered during the reigns of Uzziah, Jotham, Ahaz, and Hezekiah, kings of Judah, and in the days of Jeroboam, the son of Joash, king of Israel. So, he is dated both from the reigns of Southern and Northern kings.

Had he ministered from the first day to the last day of the reigns of these kings, his ministry would have been a century long or so. But the text does not say that; it merely says he ministered during their reigns. The great likelihood, though, is that he ministered somewhere around seventy to eighty years. That is a long time to be in the ministry today, and it was a very long time to be in the ministry back in those difficult days! Prophets in the Divided Kingdom years were as likely to end up sawed in half or stoned to death as they were to be respected and revered.

Looking back at the information that the historical books afford us, we find that economically, things were incredibly good for the people of Hosea. He was a citizen of the Northern

Kingdom, and Jeroboam II was on the throne in their capital city of Samaria. Jeroboam II recovered a great deal of territory that had been lost in previous generations; the only time the kingdom was bigger was during the reigns of David and Solomon.

And all of that is what makes the prophecies of Hosea such a staggering thing. He was prophesying judgment both on the North and the South when judgment was still so far away that no one saw any signs of its coming. He was warning of them going into captivity when it seemed as if they were once again becoming one of the great powers of the world.

So, as we study through this book, remember that it was set against a backdrop of prosperity.

A bewildering command

Hosea 1:2 *The beginning of the word of the LORD by Hosea. And the LORD said to Hosea, Go, take unto thee a wife of whoredoms and children of whoredoms: for the land hath committed great whoredom, departing from the LORD.*

This quickly in the book, we come to one of the most shocking verses in all of the Bible. And God did not work up to this point; it was His very first message through the prophet to the people: *the beginning of the word of the LORD by Hosea.*

That word was a visual message. It was Hosea doing something, expressly at God's command, that would set every tongue in the nation to wagging. God told Hosea to go and marry a woman of whoredoms who already had children from that whoredom.

As you may well imagine, this verse so scandalizes those who miss the point, that they go to marathonian lengths to try and make it mean anything other than what it actually says. Adam Clarke writes this off as "a wife from among the Israelites, who were remarkable for spiritual fornication." (Clarke, 623) The Family Bible Notes, Jamieson, Fausset, and Brown, and

John Wesley's Notes declare this to be merely something Hosea would do in a vision.

But there would be nothing at all remarkable, and certainly nothing truly scandalous, in either of those things. A vision for Hosea to relate to the people or a marriage to a fellow Israelite would be so ordinary and commonplace as to barely cause a ripple on the glassy-smooth Israeli societal waters of his day.

And God very much wanted to cause a tidal wave of reaction, not merely a bare ripple. No other prophet was yet telling the people that they were going to fall because of their sin. God wanted Hosea to both say it and, this is essential, to show them why.

And so God told Hosea to marry and love a woman that no one thought deserved to be loved and married. He told Hosea to marry a woman with a well-established reputation as an immoral woman and who had produced children through that immorality.

The main objection to this is one that also generally completely misses the point, and that is the claim that God was commanding Hosea to do something sinful. But Hosea was not the one who engaged in any whoredom; only Gomer did that. Hosea was a pure man who simply married a woman with a dirty past. Hosea never sinned a single time in what he did; he merely scandalized a nation by giving a woman who had been stained and scarred by sin a new start in life and a chance to be truly loved for the first time ever, along with her children who had done nothing to cause any of this.

And if Hosea is starting to sound a whole lot like Christ in all of this, then congratulations – you actually get the point that most others miss. Look at the last half of verse two:

Hosea 1:2b *...Go, take unto thee a wife of whoredoms and children of whoredoms: **for** the land hath committed great whoredom, departing from the LORD.*

For. God told Hosea to marry Gomer and take in her children for, because, Israel had committed great whoredom in departing from the LORD. They were rich, successful, everything seemed to be coming up roses, but God was angry with them because of their spiritual whoredom. Not to get too far ahead of ourselves, please understand that the entire picture God was going to paint through the book was of Him taking Israel in as a people when they were dirty and unworthy, taking them in as if they were His bride, and then experiencing the broken heart of having them spurn that undeserved love and commit adultery against Him. And this command for Hosea to marry Gomer was the first part of that picture. And the picture only becomes more pointed and profound when you know the meanings of the names of the people involved.

Hosea means salvation – and the New Testament rendering of the name is Jesus. Gomer means corruption. Just as the Old Testament Jesus took in a dirty bride and made something special of her, the New Testament Jesus took in a dirty bride—us Gentiles—and made something special of us. The book of Hosea is one of the most glorious pictures of Christ and the church that could ever be imagined!

But this thing of a man of God marrying a woman of ill repute still brings up questions, does it not? Especially for us, the church, the idea of a pastor ever marrying such a woman would definitely lead to an argument about whether he was truly blameless, as 1 Timothy 3:2 requires of a pastor.

But did you notice what words I did and did not use in that last paragraph? I used the word pastor twice, but, and this again is key, I did not use the word *prophet*. And those were two very different things, one of which we no longer even have today.

A pastor is a New Testament office given to a man who has the completed Scripture, all sixty-six books, to use as a message to the people. A prophet was primarily an Old

Testament office (though it did stretch a bit into New Testament times until the Scripture was completed, and will be seen again in the Tribulation Period) given to a man who himself was often the message in the absence of the completed revelation of Scripture. Put in simpler terms, the pastor speaks the message; the prophet often showed the message. And that is why we also would not expect a pastor to go out in public and lay on his left side for 390 days and then roll over and lay on his right side for forty days as Ezekiel did. The seemingly odd things that prophets like Hosea and Ezekiel did have no bearing on the New Testament pastor; they were merely living demonstrations of the Word of God during the days when the Word was not yet fully in print.

Let's focus for a moment, though, on the specific issue God had with Israel that led to the bewildering command to begin with:

Hosea 1:2 *...for the land hath committed great whoredom, departing from the LORD.*

Throughout the book, Hosea will describe in great detail the idolatry that led to this pronouncement. And it was not some isolated, minority thing. It was not something in which a few of the people were giving the rest of the people a bad name. It was the land that was committing great whoredom. There were so few even attempting to do right that it was fair to say that Israel was a people who, as a whole, had sold themselves to idolatry, much of which was still centered around Jeroboam I's golden calves in Dan and Bethel. And thus, in the face of such dramatic wickedness, God had His prophet live a picture of dramatic accusation.

A beginning to the love story

Hosea 1:3 *So he went and took Gomer the daughter of Diblaim; which conceived, and bare him a son.*

This is not a mysterious verse—but it is a breathtaking one if you truly see the details in the words.

God came to Hosea and told him to do the oddest, most unpredictable of things. He told the prophet, the man everyone looked to as an example, to go and marry a woman of ill repute. And Hosea apparently knew just the woman; everyone in Israel likely did.

Hosea made his way through the streets to the home of a man named Diblaim. Diblaim had a daughter, a daughter that did not have a good name. Diblaim likely thought that she had ruined any chance she ever had to marry a decent man. Who, after all, would want the baggage she would bring to a marriage? Imagine Diblaim's surprise, then, when he heard a knock on the front door and opened it to find Hosea, the prophet of God standing there. His heart likely fell. Was the man of God here to pronounce judgment on his child? Would she be dragged into the streets and stoned to death?

No, that is not what Hosea was there for. Diblaim may have had to sit down and say, "Could you please run that by me again?" when he heard the words "I would like permission to marry your daughter, Gomer," come out of the mouth of the prophet.

Hosea! This was God's man, a prophet who would shake two kingdoms on His behalf! And yet this sacred, reputable man was asking for his daughter's hand in marriage!

Gomer would have been just as shocked. To say that she and Hosea were from opposite sides of the track would be the theological understatement of the century. But he was not being vague or coy in his words; he was asking both father and daughter for the right to marry Gomer.

I would dearly love to have seen her reaction. I would also love to know whether she agreed at once or asked for time to consider the matter. Everyone in that house knew that she was being asked to forsake the life of a prostitute for the life of a prophet's wife.

Whether she agreed at once or took time to consider it first, she did agree. Hosea the prophet and Gomer the prostitute went through the ceremonies of the day and became man and wife. And some months later, Hosea came home to heart-pounding news: he was going to be a father. Gomer was pregnant.

This was new territory for both, but in different ways. Hosea had never been married or had children, as far as we know. And Gomer, who had had children, had never had a good and godly man by her side as her pregnancy progressed. All any men had even cared about concerning her was the physical pleasure she could offer them for a price. Hosea actually loved her. Hosea was celebrating each new milestone in the pregnancy.

Finally, delivery day came. And after who knows how many hours of pushing and struggling, a small cry was heard from the other room. Soon, a midwife came out and handed a little bundle to Hosea, saying, "Congratulations, man of God; you have a son."

She deserved none of that joy, none of that love, none of that happiness. She did not deserve to be in the family of Hosea, the family of Salvation. And yet Hosea afforded her all of it anyway.

But she isn't the only one. Not one of us deserves any of the joy, love, and happiness our Hosea, our Jesus, has afforded us. None of us deserve to be in the family of Salvation. And Yet Jesus has afforded all of that to us anyway.

Every time you read the book of Hosea, see yourself in Gomer and then thank God for the day Salvation came and knocked on your door.

Chapter Two
The Glow and the Gathering Darkness

Hosea 1:4 *And the LORD said unto him, Call his name Jezreel; for yet a little while, and I will avenge the blood of Jezreel upon the house of Jehu, and will cause to cease the kingdom of the house of Israel.* **5** *And it shall come to pass at that day, that I will break the bow of Israel in the valley of Jezreel.* **6** *And she conceived again, and bare a daughter. And God said unto him, Call her name Loruhamah: for I will no more have mercy upon the house of Israel; but I will utterly take them away.* **7** *But I will have mercy upon the house of Judah, and will save them by the LORD their God, and will not save them by bow, nor by sword, nor by battle, by horses, nor by horsemen.* **8** *Now when she had weaned Loruhamah, she conceived, and bare a son.* **9** *Then said God, Call his name Loammi: for ye are not my people, and I will not be your God.* **10** *Yet the number of the children of Israel shall be as the sand of the sea, which cannot be measured nor numbered; and it shall come to pass, that in the place where it was said unto them, Ye are not my people, there it shall be said unto them, Ye are the sons of the living God.* **11** *Then shall the children of Judah and the children of Israel be gathered together, and appoint themselves one head, and they shall come up out of the land: for great shall be the day of Jezreel.*

God had come to Hosea the prophet with the most unimaginable of commands; Hosea was to go and marry a well-known prostitute, taking in her and her children. And he did. And as we ended the last section of verses in verse three, here is what we read:

Hosea 1:3 *So he went and took Gomer the daughter of Diblaim; which conceived, and bare him a son.*

Verse four will pick the story up from the time of the birth of that son.

A shadow of the past

Hosea 1:4 *And the LORD said unto him, Call his name Jezreel; for yet a little while, and I will avenge the blood of Jezreel upon the house of Jehu, and will cause to cease the kingdom of the house of Israel.* **5** *And it shall come to pass at that day, that I will break the bow of Israel in the valley of Jezreel.*

While there is undeniably prophecy at play here, we dare not miss the fact that there was also a very real husband and wife holding their very real newborn baby boy. In the household of Hosea that day, there was a woman who had been rescued from the depths of depravity and yet was now experiencing the heights of happiness. There is no way in the world that Gomer ever expected any of this while out in her old life of sin. And yet, as she lay there holding her beautiful baby boy, it was all very real.

To describe all of this as a honeymoon period would be an understatement, especially considering how unlikely all of it was to begin with. There was doubtless a glow over the household of Hosea, the happiness that only comes from pure love brought to be by God Himself.

But there was still business to attend to. And the first order of business, an order of business attended to by parents for thousands of years, was to name the child. And Gomer was quickly to find out that the naming of the child would be as much planned and directed by God as was her union to Hosea itself. Just like God had a purpose for telling the preacher to marry the prostitute, He also had a purpose for the children that would come from that union. These children would become living representations of how things were going between God and His people.

Jezreel. God Himself spoke to Hosea and instructed him to name their new baby boy Jezreel.

This was, at once, both a very common and a very uncommon name. As far as places went, the name Jezreel was very well and very widely used in Scripture. As far as people, though, only one other person is given that name in Scripture, an individual listed in a genealogy in 1 Chronicles 4:3. So when Hosea told his wife that the boy was to be named Jezreel, there was likely a moment of confusion followed by a moment of apprehension.

And if there was apprehension on her part, she was soon to realize that it was for very good reason.

As to the name itself, Jezreel simply means "God sows." It paints the picture of one scattering or dispersing seeds. It was a name that indicated that God was very active in bringing things to be, especially where humanity was concerned, and very especially where humanity had done wrong. And that aspect of the name is exactly what God had in mind when He named that child:

Hosea 1:4 *And the LORD said unto him, Call his name Jezreel; for yet a little while, and I will avenge the blood of Jezreel upon the house of Jehu, and will cause to cease the kingdom of the house of Israel.*

Put yourself in Hosea and Gomer's place at that moment. Hosea has been called into the service of God as a prophet. But Gomer is just a wife who is trying to adjust to a new life of purity instead of her old life of sin. She has a baby that she wants to take care of and, doubtless, wants to see him grow up and live a normal life. But right off the bat, she is going to be reminded of what all of this is about to begin with. Her son is given a name that looks backward in time to a great wrong that has been done and forward in time to a great judgment that will fall in response.

The name Jezreel takes us all the way back to the time of the most wicked marital monarchy to ever disgrace the earth—Ahab and Jezebel.

Roughly one hundred years or so before the birth of this baby boy, Jezebel had brought to pass, and Ahab had been an accomplice in the murder of Naboth. And Naboth lived in a pretty familiar-sounding place:

1 Kings 21:1 *And it came to pass after these things, that Naboth the **Jezreelite** had a vineyard, which was in Jezreel, hard by the palace of Ahab king of Samaria.*

The story is pretty well known. Ahab wanted Naboth's vineyard, and Naboth rightly refused to sell it. Jezebel set him up on false charges and had him stoned to death. But God noticed what was done and had His man pronounce judgment on both of them:

1 Kings 21:17 *And the word of the LORD came to Elijah the Tishbite, saying,* **18** *Arise, go down to meet Ahab king of Israel, which is in Samaria: behold, he is in the vineyard of Naboth, whither he is gone down to possess it.* **19** *And thou shalt speak unto him, saying, Thus saith the LORD, Hast thou killed, and also taken possession? And thou shalt speak unto him, saying, Thus saith the LORD, In the place where dogs licked the blood of Naboth shall dogs lick thy blood, even thine.* **20** *And Ahab said to Elijah, Hast thou found me, O mine enemy? And he answered, I have found thee: because thou hast sold thyself to work evil in the sight of the LORD.* **21** *Behold, I will bring evil upon thee, and will take away thy posterity, and will cut off from Ahab him that pisseth against the wall, and him that is shut up* *and left in Israel,* **22** *And will make thine house like the house of Jeroboam the son of Nebat, and like the house of Baasha the son of Ahijah, for the provocation wherewith thou hast provoked me to anger, and made Israel to sin.* **23** *And of Jezebel also spake the LORD, saying, The dogs shall eat Jezebel by the wall of* **Jezreel***.*

God's judgment came to pass. But there was a very specific person by whom He made that judgment come to pass, as He told Elijah some years before. His name was Jehu, and here is where it all began to unfold as God said that it would:

2 Kings 9:25 *Then said Jehu to Bidkar his captain, Take up, and cast him* [Ahab] *in the portion of the field of Naboth the Jezreelite: for remember how that, when I and thou rode together after Ahab his father, the LORD laid this burden upon him;* **26** *Surely I have seen yesterday the blood of Naboth, and the blood of his sons, saith the LORD; and I will requite thee in this plat, saith the LORD. Now therefore take and cast him into the plat of ground, according to the word of the LORD.* **27** *But when Ahaziah the king of Judah saw this, he fled by the way of the garden house. And Jehu followed after him, and said, Smite him also in the chariot. And they did so at the going up to Gur, which is by Ibleam. And he fled to Megiddo, and died there.* **28** *And his servants carried him in a chariot to Jerusalem, and buried him in his sepulchre with his fathers in the city of David.* **29** *And in the eleventh year of Joram the son of Ahab began Ahaziah to reign over Judah.* **30** *And when Jehu was come to Jezreel, Jezebel heard of it; and she painted her face, and tired her head, and looked out at a window.* **31** *And as Jehu entered in at the gate, she said, Had Zimri peace, who slew his master?* **32** *And he lifted up his face to the window, and said, Who is on my side? who? And there looked out to him two or three eunuchs.* **33** *And he said, Throw her down. So they threw her down: and some of her blood was sprinkled on the wall, and on the horses: and he trode her under foot.* **34** *And when he was come in, he* *did eat and drink, and said, Go, see now this cursed woman, and bury her: for she is a king's daughter.* **35** *And they went to bury her: but they found no more of her than the skull, and the feet, and the palms of her hands.* **36** *Wherefore they came again, and told him. And he said, This is the word of the LORD, which he spake by his servant Elijah the Tishbite, saying, In the portion of **Jezreel** shall dogs eat the flesh of Jezebel:*

Jehu went on to wipe out the royal house of Ahab. And here is where things get pretty interesting as we study the book of Hosea. Look again at what God said concerning this:

Hosea 1:4 *And the LORD said unto him, Call his name Jezreel; for yet a little while, and I will avenge the blood of Jezreel upon the house of Jehu, and will cause to cease the kingdom of the house of Israel.*

God told Jehu to wipe out the house of Ahab, and he did. So why, then, one hundred years or so later, did God determine to judge the house of Jehu and even the whole kingdom of Israel on that account?

What Jehu did, he did not out of allegiance to and worship of God, but out of bloodthirstiness and cruelty; the pride and arrogance with which he reigned afterward proved this. And his household, far from turning away from the wickedness of previous kings, embraced the very wickedness of Jeroboam I and his golden calves, the wickedness that started it all in the North (2 Kings 10:29-31) and continued to live in it and promote it to others. In fact, Jeroboam II, the wicked king on the throne during the days of Hosea, was of the line of Jehu.

God often judges wicked people by means of other wicked people, but that never means that He approves of either set of those wicked people. And wickedness will always bear a cost that must at some point be paid.

Back to the household of Gomer and Hosea, though, Gomer is now learning that her precious baby boy will bear a name that looks back to the wickedness of her people and ahead to the destruction of her people. And that destruction would happen in a very particular place:

Hosea 1:5 *And it shall come to pass at that day, that I will break the bow of Israel in the valley of **Jezreel**.*

Hosea may not have realized it, but he would live to see the fulfillment of this prophecy that he now uttered through the name of his son. Some forty years later, Jezreel, also known as the great plain of Esdraelon, became the site of Shalmaneser's victory over Israel at Beth-arbel. In the words of Charles L. Feinberg, "This was the last dread admonition from God before the fall of Samaria." (Feinberg, 17)

A separation of destiny

Hosea 1:6a *And she conceived again, and bare a daughter.*

Let's stop for just a moment to consider the timeline. Hosea and Gomer have now been married long enough to have two children born to them. Considering the time of mandatory separation and purification after the birth of a child, they have been married for, at the very least, two years or so, perhaps considerably longer. Two years of time to settle into a marriage. Two years of time to love and laugh and fight and make up. Two years of time to go through the joy of seeing two lives grow in the womb. Two years of time for her to be a homemaker rather than a harlot, a cherished bride rather than a cheap diversion.

And now both Hosea and Gomer were hearing the words, "Congratulations, it's a girl!"

So now, along with the other children that had been brought into the marriage of which we will speak in further verses, there is a boy and a girl that has been born to Mr. and Mrs. Hosea.

Gomer was likely a bit nervous; when their first child was born, their baby boy, he was given a name that people around them would cringe at every time they heard it.

She had good reason to be nervous; the name of the second child would be loaded with prophetical import as well:

Hosea 1:6 *And she conceived again, and bare a daughter. And God said unto him, Call her name Loruhamah: for I will no more have mercy upon the house of Israel; but I will utterly take them away.*

Jezreel was a rare name for a person, being given to only one other in Scripture. Loruhamah, though, was rarer still; this child would be the only one in all of Scripture to have that name.

Loruhamah means "no more mercy."

By now, everyone knew that Hosea's marriage to Gomer and all of the children to come from it had prophetical significance concerning the nation. After the first child, everyone knew that God's intent was to judge Israel for a century of sin beginning with Ahab, Jezebel, and Jehu. Now, with the second child, they were to realize how serious that judgment would be: it would be a judgment utterly without mercy.

Concerning this, God said of Israel at the end of verse six that he would *utterly take them away*. Unlike Judah, which was restored as a kingdom after seventy years of captivity in Babylon, Israel experienced no such restoration. Bits and pieces of all the tribes made their way back to the land through the years, becoming part of what Judah was rebuilding, but the Northern Kingdom ceased to exist the day that Assyria overran them for the final time.

On the prophetical side, the power of God should astound us; no one could have seen this coming in the days when Hosea was uttering the prophecy.

On the personal side, the household of Hosea and Gomer should concern us; how would they do through having another child whose very name was going to bring scorn and ridicule?

There was, though, a silver lining to this gathering cloud:

Hosea 1:7 *But I will have mercy upon the house of Judah, and will save them by the LORD their God, and will not save them by bow, nor by sword, nor by battle, by horses, nor by horsemen.*

God both was and was not going to have mercy. His mercy with Israel, the Northern Kingdom, had run out. For the entirety of their history, they had not a single good and godly king, and pursued their idols with passion. Judah, though, had many good kings scattered amongst their bad kings and many revivals scattered throughout their reprobacy. Because of this, the mercy of God would extend for another 136 years to the Southern Kingdom. And in verse seven, Hosea prophesied a specific instance of that mercy, a time when God was going to save Judah from destruction by His own power, not by bow or sword or battle or horses or horsemen. And in a large amount of salt to the wound for the Northern Kingdom, it would be the very Assyrians that carried them into captivity that God stopped in their tracks as a show of mercy to Judah.

Here is where and how that happened:

2 Kings 19:35 *And it came to pass that night, that the angel of the LORD went out, and smote in the camp of the Assyrians an hundred fourscore and five thousand: and when they arose early in the morning, behold, they were all dead corpses.* **36** *So Sennacherib king of Assyria departed, and went and returned, and dwelt at Nineveh.*

The same God that did this for Judah could have done the same thing for Israel. Israel, though, had pushed beyond His last measure of mercy, and Loruhama was a crying, wiggling, growing testimony of that every day of her young life.

A sentence of judgment

Hosea 1:8a *Now when she had weaned Loruhamah, she conceived, and bare a son.*

Let us once again examine the timeline as we see how things are going in the house of Hosea and Gomer. When last we saw them, they had been married for at least two years and were celebrating the birth of their second child. And now we find that after she had weaned that second child, she conceived and bore a third child, a baby boy.

The weaning of a child in those days and in that part of the world was, on average, at around three years old, though in some cases it could be even a year or two longer than that. But just looking at it from the perspective of the normal three-year period of time, we have the at least two-year period of time we have already examined plus the three years of weaning plus another year for purification and conception and nine months later the birth of this third child.

So by this point, Hosea and Gomer have been married for six years or so. Six years of time to settle into a marriage. Six years of time to love and laugh and fight and make up. Six years of time to go through the joy of seeing three lives grow in the womb. Six years of time for her to be a homemaker rather than a harlot, a cherished bride rather than a cheap diversion. Six years for her to understand how much God loves her and how much Hosea loves her and how much better off she has it now than she had it in her old life of sin.

She also, though, surely knows by now what is coming when it comes to the naming of this child:

Hosea 1:9 *Then said God, Call his name Loammi: for ye are not my people, and I will not be your God.*

After this many years of marriage to the prophet of God, one could hope that Gomer has truly bought into all of it, having learned both the word of God and the ways of God.

As we will see at the beginning of chapter two, though, that was not the case.

As to the naming of this child, though, his name, Loammi, is every bit as rare as the name of his sister, Loruhamah. He is the only one in Scripture that ever carried this name, and it means "not my people."

If you have ever uttered the pointed little phrase, "not my circus, not my monkeys," then you are beginning to scratch the surface of the sentiment of this name. God was looking at people who had always been His people and telling them that He no longer regarded them as such. He was, in our vernacular, disowning them.

But this begs a rather particular question, does it not? The covenant that God made with Abraham in Genesis 12 and 15 was an absolutely unconditional covenant. And hundreds of years later, in Romans 11:1-2a, Paul said, "I say then, Hath God cast away his people? God forbid. For I also am an Israelite, of the seed of Abraham, of the tribe of Benjamin. God hath not cast away his people which he foreknew..."

How, then, are we to reconcile this difficulty?

Feinberg gave a wonderful explanation of this, saying:

> "The Abrahamic covenant stands fast and sure, no matter what Israel does. First and last, it is an unconditional covenant. This makes Abraham's seed always God's chosen people. But they must be in obedience and following the will of the Lord before they can have this experimentally realized in their lives. When they depart from the way of the Lord and are dealt with by God in chastisement, they appear for all intents and purposes to be "Not My People," Lo-ammi. When they return to God through Christ in the coming day, they will be in fact what they

have always been in the counsels of God."
(Feinberg, 17)

Let me put it this way in simpler form. Just like salvation, in God's covenant with Israel there is a difference between the positional and the practical. Positionally, both Israel as a nation and individual Christians as born-again children of God will always be His people. Practically, though, both they and we can remove ourselves from His blessings and favor through the way that we live our lives.

And that is exactly what God was indicating through Hosea to the people by naming this child Loammi. While in their relationship with God they would always be His people, in their fellowship with God they were now anything but and would be dealt with as such. They were going to experience His blisterings rather than His blessings and to such a degree that no one would ever even believe they actually were His people.

A surety of restoration

Hosea 1:10 *Yet the number of the children of Israel shall be as the sand of the sea, which cannot be measured nor numbered; and it shall come to pass, that in the place where it was said unto them, Ye are not my people, there it shall be said unto them, Ye are the sons of the living God.*

Through everything that we are reading, please remember that the education of Gomer was still taking place within all of it. She has just been informed that her third child's name is to be Loammi, and that it means that God no longer regards Israel as His people.

But then, at the beginning of verse ten, she hears the most remarkable little word—"yet."

Oh, what unfathomable hope is found in that tiny word!

And how everyone's heart must have leaped as they heard the rest:

Hosea 1:10 *Yet the number of the children of Israel shall be as the sand of the sea, which cannot be measured nor numbered;*

Hosea was telling everyone that God took Israel in when she was unworthy, and that she had committed spiritual adultery against Him, and that He was going to allow Assyria to completely overrun her. She was no longer even going to be regarded as being His people. But the very next thing God told him to say was that yet, in spite of all that, the number of the children of Israel would be as the sand of the sea which cannot be measured or numbered. And this wording comes directly from the words that God gave as a covenant to Abraham and his grandson, Jacob:

Genesis 22:17 *That in blessing I will bless thee, and in multiplying I will multiply thy seed as the stars of the heaven, and as the sand which is upon the sea shore; and thy seed shall possess the gate of his enemies;*

Genesis 32:12 *And thou saidst, I will surely do thee good, and make thy seed as the sand of the sea, which cannot be numbered for multitude.*

This is a perfect indication of what we just covered—the fact that God's covenant with Abraham is absolutely unconditional, so that even when they are "not His people" practically, they still very much are His people positionally, and as such, every promise He has ever made them is sure.

The anti-Semites of the world need to understand this: no matter how bad they hate it, Israel is never going away.

Look again at verse ten, now focusing very particularly on the last half of it:

Hosea 1:10b *...and it shall come to pass, that in the place where it was said unto them, Ye are not my people, there it shall be said unto them, Ye are the sons of the living God.*

This is more significant than you may realize. It is not just that Israel is always going to exist as a people, it is that in the very place where God told them, "ye are not my people," people would eventually be saying to them, "ye are the sons of the living God."

God spoke those words to them in the land of Israel before they were dispersed into Assyria. And then for 1800 or more years, they along with Judah were disbursed from the land at the hands of Rome in 136 A. D. And yet it was to that very land that God, against all human reason, brought them back and established them as a people in 1948. They are now multiplying and thriving there once again, and it is in and around their existence and that very land that all of the events of the Tribulation Period will unfold. It is with them in that very land that Christ their King will reign on the throne of his father David for a thousand years.

Israel the people will always be, and Israel the land will always belong to her.

But there is still one more part to that amazing promise:

Hosea 1:11 *Then shall the children of Judah and the children of Israel be gathered together, and appoint themselves one head, and they shall come up out of the land: for great shall be the day of Jezreel.*

When Hosea wrote these words, the children of Judah and the children of Israel had already been separated for around 150 years. As he was writing those words, the separation was about to get even more profound, with Israel about to fall to Assyria and be dispersed.

But the promise of God was that one day, there would be the grandest of reunions. One day, the ten tribes and the two tribes would once again be one nation of twelve tribes. One day, rather than having separate kings, they would have one head. And interestingly, verse eleven says that they would appoint themselves this one head. And while all of that applies in the barest of forms to the days after both the Assyrian and Babylonian captivities were ended and Zerubbabel the governor led them all, God was ultimately pointing to something much greater and farther afield than that. He was pointing to the day when all of His people would with one heart and mind willingly coronate their true King, Jesus, to rule over them.

As verse eleven describes, on that day, they will "come up out of the land." All during the Tribulation Period, they will be fleeing to the wilderness ahead of those determined to destroy them. But when their one true King destroys all of their enemies, they will come out of the land and back to their capital city. Hosea describes all of this at the end of verse eleven this way: *for great shall be the day of Jezreel.*

Jezreel—God sows, God disperses. Great indeed will be the day when God sows wrath and judgment and disperses, casts to the winds, those who have sought to destroy His people!

Six years. For six years, God used this marriage between the prophet and the former prostitute and the children that they produced as man and wife to send a message to His people. And much of that message was a decidedly and necessarily negative message. True, it ended positively, but for the house of Hosea and Gomer, there was this mixture of the glow and the gathering darkness.

And none of that was God's fault.

God was not the one that caused Israel to stray, and God was not the one that caused Gomer to sell her body. Instead, God was the one who loved Israel anyway and had Hosea do the same for Gomer.

And both Israel and Gomer were going to have to make a choice as to what they would do with that undeserved love.

Everyone ultimately has to make that same choice.

Chapter Three
Broken Home, Broken Heart

Hosea 2:1 *Say ye unto your brethren, Ammi; and to your sisters, Ruhamah.* **2** *Plead with your mother, plead: for she is not my wife, neither am I her husband: let her therefore put away her whoredoms out of her sight, and her adulteries from between her breasts;* **3** *Lest I strip her naked, and set her as in the day that she was born, and make her as a wilderness, and set her like a dry land, and slay her with thirst.* **4** *And I will not have mercy upon her children; for they be the children of whoredoms.* **5** *For their mother hath played the harlot: she that conceived them hath done shamefully: for she said, I will go after my lovers, that give me my bread and my water, my wool and my flax, mine oil and my drink.* **6** *Therefore, behold, I will hedge up thy way with thorns, and make a wall, that she shall not find her paths.* **7** *And she shall follow after her lovers, but she shall not overtake them; and she shall seek them, but shall not find them: then shall she say, I will go and return to my first husband; for then was it better with me than now.* **8** *For she did not know that I gave her corn, and wine, and oil, and multiplied her silver and gold, which they prepared for Baal.* **9** *Therefore will I return, and take away my corn in the time thereof, and my wine in the season thereof, and will recover my wool and my flax given to cover her nakedness.* **10** *And now will I discover her lewdness in the sight of her lovers, and none shall deliver her out of mine hand.* **11** *I* *will also cause all her mirth to cease, her feast days, her new moons, and her sabbaths, and all her solemn feasts.* **12** *And I will destroy her vines and her fig trees, whereof she hath said, These are my rewards that my lovers have given me: and I will make them a forest, and the beasts of the field shall eat them.* **13** *And I will visit upon her the days of Baalim, wherein she burned incense to them, and she decked herself with her earrings and her jewels, and she went after her lovers, and forgat me, saith the LORD.*

As chapter one of the book of Hosea ended, there was a glow in the household of Hosea and Gomer. They had at least six years of marriage behind them, long enough to have high hopes that Gomer really was changed and that all would be well. They also had three children together, two boys and one girl.

But the names Hosea gave the children at God's command were a reminder that judgment was coming on Israel, and Hosea's family was to be a testimony to that. So yes, there was a glow, but there was also a gathering darkness.

And in chapter two, it was about to erupt into a full-blown storm.

A family splintered

Hosea 2:1 *Say ye unto your brethren, Ammi; and to your sisters, Ruhamah.* **2a** *Plead with your mother, plead: for she is not my wife, neither am I her husband...*

We are given no indication as to the ages of Hosea and Gomer when they were married. Nor are we given any information as to how long they were married before the splintering of the home began to occur. But as Hosea begins to speak in verse one of this chapter, it is interesting that he addresses the two youngest children that he and Gomer had together but does not mention Jezreel, the oldest. And that omission becomes even more stark in the light of the fact that the name Jezreel will only be mentioned one more time in Scripture—and that it is at the end of this very chapter. And looking at that mention seems to give us a clue as to the fate of Jezreel:

Hosea 2:22 *And the earth shall hear the corn, and the wine, and the oil; and they shall hear Jezreel.*

This verse deals with future prophecy. And yet, it deals with future prophecy in the light of the present circumstance of Hosea and Gomer. It seems, then, that they were no longer hearing Jezreel by the time of the splintering of the home—he likely had passed away. This would explain why Hosea pleads with his youngest children to plead with their mother, but not with the first child that they had together.

We also find in verse one, though, a reference to the children that Gomer brought with her into the marriage. Remember what God commanded Hosea at the very outset:

Hosea 1:2 *The beginning of the word of the LORD by Hosea. And the LORD said to Hosea, Go, take unto thee a wife of whoredoms and children of whoredoms: for the land hath committed great whoredom, departing from the LORD.*

Gomer brought children, plural, into the marriage, children that she had conceived by her whoredoms. And we now know that there were at least three of them by the numbers given to us at the beginning of chapter two:

Hosea 2:1 *Say ye unto your brethren, Ammi; and to your sisters, Ruhamah.*

We are given the names of three children that Hosea and Gomer had together. But we find at least six children in this verse; Ammi had at least two brothers, and Ruhamah had at least two sisters. These other children will be mentioned specifically and caustically in verse four of this chapter.

Another interesting family note that we find in the first verse of this chapter, though, is that Hosea was referring to his other two children by nicknames, as it were. The proper names of those children were Loruhama and Loammi; No more mercy, and Not my people. But though Hosea obeyed the Lord and gave them those names, it seems that in the home, the heart of this father could not bring itself to refer to those precious children by those names. As he pleads with them from the emotions of his heart, he removes the prefix of each and calls them Ruhama and Ammi; mercy, and my people.

And it truly was an hour for emotion, not merely instruction. Here, again, is what was happening in the home:

Hosea 2:2a *Plead with your mother, plead: for she is not my wife, neither am I her husband...*

As we will see in the text to come, Gomer had abandoned her husband and children in order to pursue her former life of sin. And thus it is that we find a brokenhearted father twice imploring his children to plead with their mother. While they were still technically married, her abandonment and adultery had produced a situation in which, for all practical purposes, she was no longer Hosea's wife, nor was Hosea her husband.

Although God never makes such a thing happen, God knew that all of this would transpire. It was, in fact, one of the very reasons why He commanded Hosea to marry Gomer to begin with. Just as Hosea took in an unworthy woman and loved her with an unfathomable love, God took in Israel as an unworthy people and loved her with an unfathomable love as well. Just as Gomer spurned that unfathomable love and pursued actual whoredom instead, Israel also spurned that unfathomable love and pursued spiritual whoredom, chasing after false gods and idols on every corner.

And just as it broke the heart of Hosea, it also broke the heart of God.

A familiar sin

Hosea 2:2b ...*let her therefore put away her whoredoms out of her sight, and her adulteries from between her breasts;*

The language in which Hosea spoke to his children and God spoke to His people in these words is both plain and picturesque. Gomer was seeing her lovers; they were constantly in her sight. Gomer was embracing her lovers, letting them see and experience things that were only designed for her husband.

Gomer did not abandon Hosea and become a witch or a murderer or a robber; she ran back to the sin with which she had always been the most familiar: whoredom.

Israel did not abandon God and become atheists; she ran back to the sin with which she had always been the most familiar: the polytheism and idolatry she had been so familiar with from the days of Egypt.

Occasionally, you may find a believer who backslides on God into some brand-new sin. But the vast majority of the time, nearly all the time, really, people who backslide will backslide into the very sin they came out of, the thing with which they are the most familiar, the thing their flesh still craves and calls for. It is for this very reason we must always walk so very close to God and be filled with the Holy Spirit and set strong boundaries for our flesh.

A fearful sentence

Hosea had pled with his children to plead with their mother. It seems that, as is so often the case, the mother who had abandoned the home was still willing to talk with her children even though she wanted nothing to do with the man who fathered them.

And now, Hosea began to explain to his children what he was planning and what they needed to communicate to her.

Hosea 2:3 *Lest I strip her naked, and set her as in the day that she was born, and make her as a wilderness, and set her like a dry land, and slay her with thirst.*

What Hosea proposed to do here would be done, in our vernacular, with his checkbook, not with his hands. As he will explain in verses to come, he had provided everything for her since the day that he had taken her in. He is now going to remove all of that financial support from her, which will ultimately result in her being as naked as the day she was born, as avoided as a wilderness, completely dried up, and dying of thirst. And if all of that somehow sounds harsh, then you have completely missed the point:

Absolutely none of it was necessary.

All she ever had to do to have Hosea take care of her forever was stay home and fulfill her vows. All of the clothing and food and water for Gomer was still available; but it was available at home, not in the cheap rooms in which she was laying around with other men. She had no right whatsoever to expect her husband to continue to provide for her when she was not behaving as a wife.

Some years ago, a young gentleman came to me for counseling. His wife had left him for another man—a "friend" of his, actually. But she had left in the car that he, the husband, was still making payments on and still paying the insurance for. The car had then broken down. She called him to let him know he needed to have it towed to a shop for repairs and that she would let him know when it was done so that he could pay for those repairs... so that she could continue to use it to cheat on him.

Let all of that sink in.

My counsel was that he behave exactly like Hosea, and have the car towed back into his own driveway, turn in the tag, and drop the insurance on it. I also counseled him to stop paying for her cell phone—the phone she used to make the plans to meet up with her adulterous boyfriend. I counseled him to cut off absolutely all financial support entirely. If someone is going to commit adultery, they need to do so on their own dime, not the dime of the spouse they have so violated.

This is what Hosea proposed to do to Gomer. But it is also, in a broader sense, exactly what God proposed to do to Israel. The God who had provided for them since He made them a people was going to withdraw that support until they were naked and dry and busted.

Hosea 2:4 *And I will not have mercy upon her children; for they be the children of whoredoms.*

If this verse were merely a statement that Hosea was going to be petty and vindictive to the children that Gomer brought into the marriage because of what their mother did, it would not speak well of Hosea at all. But there is far more to it than that. When they are described here as the children of whoredoms, the wording used is an indication that they were like their mother in their mentality and beliefs and conduct.

Keil and Delitzsch put it this way, "They are called the sons of whoredom not merely on account of their origin as begotten in whoredom, but also because they inherit the nature and conduct of their mother." (Keil, 53)

Hosea was telling the children who actually cared to speak to the other children and remind them that his kindness had not merely extended to their mother, it had extended to them as well. And yet, since they were now apparently in approval of their mother's choice of becoming an adulteress once again and heading that way themselves, they needed to understand that they would also be deprived of his mercy along with her.

The nation of Israel, as if the spouse of God, had committed adultery against Him with their idolatry. But the individual members of that nation, the children, if you will, were going to find themselves deprived of the mercy of God as well, both because of their involvement and even merely their approval of what was happening.

Hosea 2:5 *For their mother hath played the harlot: she that conceived them hath done shamefully: for she said, I will go after my lovers, that give me my bread and my water, my wool and my flax, mine oil and my drink.*

The words *their mother*, spoken of the children that Gomer brought into the marriage with her, are very instructive. Hosea was speaking *to* the children that he had produced along with Gomer *about* the other children that had previously been produced by Gomer. He calls her "their mother" because her behavior has now reverted back to behavior that produced them from whoredom to begin with. And this provides a salient point to consider: all of the children had a choice to make.

Amongst the nation of Israel, some chose to follow God, and some chose to follow idols. Israel, the nation, was the mother of them all. The God of Israel was the father of some of them, and that could be discerned by the choices they made and the behavior they exhibited.

But back to Gomer, what exactly was it that she had done? Here it is again:

Hosea 2:5 *For their mother hath played the harlot: she that conceived them hath done shamefully: for she said, I will go after my lovers, that give me my bread and my water, my wool and my flax, mine oil and my drink.*

At some point in their relationship, Gomer, who through the pure mercy of God and Hosea had been rescued from a life of prostitution, chose to go back to that life. On some particular and fateful day, perhaps Hosea saw it coming, perhaps he did not, she told him, *I will go after my lovers, that give me my bread and my water, my wool and my flax, mine oil and my drink.*

Gomer lacked absolutely nothing while living in the home of Hosea. In fact, in the list that will be given in the next few verses, we will find that she was given far more than there than she was seeking for elsewhere.

Gomer wanted what she wanted, and what she wanted was her lovers, plural. What she wanted was to not have anyone tell her what she could or could not do. What she wanted was no one to "judge her." What she wanted was to sleep with people and receive a price from it. She was the perfect picture of Israel who had it so very good when they were faithful to God, and yet chose to forsake that in pursuit of the wicked desires of her heart.

She is still a perfect picture of people today who do the same. But there was and is a price to pay for that choice: the deprivation of God's mercy and provision.

There was something else, though, something that Gomer would have regarded as judgment but was in fact a blessing from God:

Hosea 2:6 *Therefore, behold, I will hedge up thy way with thorns, and make a wall, that she shall not find her paths.*

For Hosea, this was a picturesque way to say that he would make Gomer's life and the pursuit of her sin as difficult as possible. He had the influence and the finances to make it seem as if every day for her was harder than the previous day, and she could make no progress. And this provides needed guidance for a spouse who is experiencing the heartbreak of Hosea in his or her own life. Any barriers and roadblocks that you can throw up in the way, any thorns that you can put in that wrong path, anything that you can rightly do to make life miserable for your adulterous spouse is a good thing. No one should ever be able to easily and comfortably commit adultery.

For Israel, this was a frightening sentence. The words that God had Hosea speak and pen in this verse very much came true through the Assyrian captivity. Would she follow after Jeroboam's golden calves? Then God would send her to a place where they were not, a place where Asshur and Ishtar were worshipped. Would she commit idolatry in freedom? Then He would send her into a place where she must do so once again in captivity.

And very few ever returned from that fate.

A focus spreading

For the rest of chapter two, the focus is gradually going to expand until it is almost entirely off of Gomer and on Israel. But verse seven will start with the focus still largely on Gomer.

Hosea 2:7 *And she shall follow after her lovers, but she shall not overtake them; and she shall seek them, but shall not find them: then shall she say, I will go and return to my first husband; for then was it better with me than now.*

Because of the barriers that Hosea was going to throw up in her pathway, Gomer was going to find herself following after her lovers but not being able to overtake them, seeking them but not being able to find them. Hosea was going to make her pursuit of her sin very difficult and, in the process, make her adulterous lovers wary of her and desirous of avoiding her, not wanting the trouble that she was unwillingly bringing with her.

His prediction as to how this was going to turn out was that she would finally come to the place where she would say, *I will go and return to my first husband; for then was it better with me than now.*

The word *first* that she would use to describe Hosea is from the word *rishone,* and it indicates something that is primary, something that is first, something that is the head, something that is chief. Gomer had despised her husband and walked out on him. But there would come a day when she would see him for the incredible man that he was and want to come back. There would come a day when she realized that things were far better with her as Hosea's wife than they were as every random man's one-night stand.

The world loves to scoff at marriage as some outdated relic of bygone days. But the miserable, lonely, childless older adults that are coming from that belief system stand in stark contrast to the happy, loved, surrounded-by-family adults of those who did it God's way.

What Israel as a nation was to learn from this, though, was that they really did have it better when they looked only to God and never cast their eyes and affections toward idols.

Hosea 2:8 *For she did not know that I gave her corn, and wine, and oil, and multiplied her silver and gold, which they prepared for Baal.* **9** *Therefore will I return, and take away my corn in the time thereof, and my wine in the season thereof, and will recover my wool and my flax given to cover her nakedness.*

The dual references to Gomer and Israel continue in this passage, though Gomer is less and less in view and Israel more and more. In verse five, Gomer had lamented the loss of bread and water and wool and flax and oil and drink (strong drink. KD, P.54) that her lovers had given her before she married Hosea. But here in verses eight and nine, we find that Hosea had given her corn and wine and oil, vast quantities of silver and gold, and also wool and flax.

Let's put that in list form to help you get a visual of it:

Her lovers gave her:	Hosea gave her:
• Bread	• Corn
• Water	• Wine
• Wool	• Oil
• Flax	• Silver
• Oil	• Gold
• Drink (strong drink)	• Wool
	• Flax

Clearly, Hosea was treating her better than her adulterous lovers did! And yet, verse eight starts with the words, *For she did not know..*

How is that even possible? Put simply, corrupt passion is the enemy of clear perception. You will more likely be successful in helping a brick wall to understand trigonometry than you will be in convincing a sinner or backslidden Christian that God is better for them and to them than the life they are building in their sin.

Find a drunk on the street shivering and covered in their own vomit, tell them how much better it would be to get saved and become a total abstainer and be in church every time the doors are open, and you will be met with laughter and profanity.

Find a fornicator wasting their years in the pursuit of sexual pleasure, explain to them how much better it would be to get married and be faithful and raise children, and you will be insulted and threatened and cursed.

Find a homosexual damaging their own body by their perverted behavior, explain how much safer and more pleasant things are when we observe God's natural order, and you will experience a torrent of hatred and blasphemy directed toward you and your God.

All you have done is state the obvious. All Hosea did was state the obvious. But she "did not know." Nor, apparently, did she consider what they were doing with the gifts that Hosea had given to her that she had then inexplicably lavished upon her lovers—who were supposedly giving her so much:

Hosea 2:8 *For she did not know that I gave her corn, and wine, and oil, and multiplied her silver and gold, which they prepared for Baal.*

The good things that Hosea gave Gomer she gave to others, who then used them in the worship of Baal. The good things that God gave Israel, she turned and used in the worship of Baal. No good thing that God ever gives is regarded as off-limits by the devil.

But God does not take the misuse of His resources lightly. Nor did Hosea. And in the next five verses He will use some form of "I will" seven times to describe how He will respond.

Hosea 2:9 *Therefore **will I** return, and take away my corn in the time thereof, and my wine in the season thereof, and **will** recover my wool and my flax given to cover her nakedness.*

Hosea was going to return—but not in a pleasant way. He was going to find Gomer and retrieve the resources that he had given to her. He was going to make her poor, and therefore unable to make herself attractive to her lovers.

God was going to retrieve the resources that He had given to His people. He was going to make them poor, and therefore unable to make themselves attractive to their idols.

Hosea 2:10 *And now **will I** discover her lewdness in the sight of her lovers, and none shall deliver her out of mine hand.*

Keil and Delitzsch do an excellent job explaining what God intends to do in this verse:

"Before the eyes of the lovers, not so that they shall be obliged to look at it, without being able to avoid it, but so that the woman shall become even to them an object of abhorrence, from which they will turn away." (Keil, 57)

Hosea was going to use every means in his power to expose Gomer for what she really was and to make even her adulterous lovers despise her.

God was going to use every means in His power to expose Israel for what she really was, and to make even her idolatrous lovers despise her.

Gomer had obviously spent years being one of the most attractive and desirable diversions for men. But that kind of a lifestyle, once it becomes fully known and aired out for all the world to see, ruins the very person who reveled in it. Would Gomer be a prostitute? Then Hosea would make her a very notable one. He would make it to where she could not so much as walk the street without mothers making their children look away and wives stepping between her and their husbands. He would expose her lewdness, verse eleven, and that is from the word *nablooth,* meaning shamelessness and immodesty. What she desired to be in the shadows before a few, he would make her in the light of day before everyone.

Hosea 2:11 *I will also cause all her mirth to cease, her feast days, her new moons, and her sabbaths, and all her solemn feasts.*

The beginning of verse eleven deals both with Gomer and Israel. The end of verse eleven begins to fade away from Gomer and focus on Israel.

As to Gomer, it was Hosea's plan to cause all of her mirth to cease. His plan was to make sure that she could not be happy in her sin. His plan was to make her miserable with her adulterous lovers. And far from being an unkindness, it is perhaps the greatest kindness of all. Helping people to enjoy their sin ensures that sinners will always reject the gospel and end up in hell for eternity, and backslidden Christians will be terrified and humiliated at the Judgment Seat of Christ.

God intended the same thing for Israel, His people. He planned to cause all of her mirth to cease; He did not want them enjoying their wickedness. But He also planned on causing some very surprising things to cease along with that joy. Look at that verse again:

Hosea 2:11 *I will also cause all her mirth to cease, her feast days, her new moons, and her sabbaths, and all her solemn feasts.*

Much of what He described here was straight from the mouth of God and the law of Moses. John Wesley said of this:

"Though apostate, Israel was fallen to idolatry, yet they retained many of the Mosaic rites and ceremonies. Her solemn feasts - The three annual feasts of tabernacles, weeks, and passover, all which ceased when they were carried captive, by Salmaneser." (Linder: John Wesley's Notes)

Did God establish those feast days and new moons and Sabbaths and solemn feasts? Yes. But did He want their joyful worship while they were equally joyful in wickedness? No. And if He had to remove the worship along with the wickedness, He would gladly do so as motivation for them to reject the wickedness and to return to actual worship.

Hosea 2:12 *And **I will** destroy her vines and her fig trees, whereof she hath said, These are my rewards that my lovers have given me: and **I will** make them a forest, and the beasts of the field shall eat them.*

Israel is almost entirely in view now. God had granted them a good land, a fertile land, and she now regarded those fruits and blessings as being the rewards of her lovers, her idols. Adam Clark said, "They attributed all the blessings of Providence as rewards received from the idols which they worshipped." (Clarke, 626)

So God determined to destroy all of those blessings. He determined to wreck her vines and her fig trees. He determined to turn her gardens into an unmanaged forest that the beasts of the field would devour.

Some of the greatest curses are the things that used to be blessings and become ruined through man's sinfulness. No dagger to the heart could be more painful to the adulterer or adulteress who has lost their family than a simple picture of the family before it was wrecked.

Hosea 2:13 *And **I will** visit upon her the days of Baalim, wherein she burned incense to them, and she decked herself with* *her earrings and her jewels, and she went after her lovers, and forgat me, saith the LORD.*

Israel is now entirely in view. The bride in this verse did not forget Hosea; she forgot the LORD. And God determined to *visit upon her* [Israel] *the days of Baalim.* When you see the designation Baal in the Bible, it is in the singular. When the im is added to the end of it, it indicates the plurality of the Baals. You see, multiple nations and tribes had their own version of Baal: Baal-Zebub, Baal-Peor, Baal-Zephon, Baal-Berith and others. Israel worshipped them all, it seems. And God was not going to put up with it. When He said that He determined to *visit upon her the days of Baalim,* visit signifies to inflict punishment. (Clarke, 626).

It is as if God was going to show up at her Baal parties and wreck everything in sight. And why would He do this? Because that is where *she burned incense to them, and she decked herself with her earrings and her jewels, and she went after her lovers, and forgat me, saith the LORD.* She was so enamored with her sin that she threw herself at her lovers and forgot the LORD.

Nothing makes a person as forgetful of God as indulging the sinful pleasures of their flesh.

Gomer had it all. She deserved none of it, but she had it all. She had a wonderful and godly husband, a house full of kids, and all the material goods that she would ever need. But the one thing that she did not have was access to her sin, because no good husband would ever put up with that while still providing all of those blessings.

Israel had it all. She deserved none of it, but she had it all. She had a God who loved her, a growing nation full of children in her own land, and all of the material goods that she would ever need. But the one thing that she did not have access to was her sin, because no holy God would ever put up with that while still providing all of those blessings.

    Gomer had a choice to make. Israel had a choice to make. We have a choice to make.

    It would be a wonderful idea to make the right choice.

Chapter Four
A Door of Hope

Hosea 2:14 *Therefore, behold, I will allure her, and bring her into the wilderness, and speak comfortably unto her.* **15** *And I will give her her vineyards from thence, and the valley of Achor for a door of hope: and she shall sing there, as in the days of her youth, and as in the day when she came up out of the land of Egypt.* **16** *And it shall be at that day, saith the LORD, that thou shalt call me Ishi; and shalt call me no more Baali.* **17** *For I will take away the names of Baalim out of her mouth, and they shall no more be remembered by their name.* **18** *And in that day will I make a covenant for them with the beasts of the field, and with the fowls of heaven, and with the creeping things of the ground: and I will break the bow and the sword and the battle out of the earth, and will make them to lie down safely.* **19** *And I will betroth thee unto me for ever; yea, I will betroth thee unto me in righteousness, and in judgment, and in lovingkindness, and in mercies.* **20** *I will even betroth thee unto me in faithfulness: and thou shalt know the LORD.* **21** *And it shall come to pass in that day, I will hear, saith the LORD, I will hear the heavens, and they shall hear the earth;* **22** *And the earth shall hear the corn, and the wine, and the oil; and they shall hear Jezreel.* **23** *And I will sow her unto me in the earth; and I will have mercy upon her that had not obtained mercy; and I will say* *to them which were not my people, Thou art my people; and they shall say, Thou art my God.*

When last we looked in on the home of Hosea and Gomer, Gomer had deserted it and the family—husband, her children, their children. She had gone back to her life of prostitution and was chasing after her lovers and the price they paid her. Hosea, for his part, was pleading with the children to plead with their mother. He genuinely wanted the marriage to be reconciled and the home to be set right.

In order to do that, he informed his children that he was going to make her life as difficult as possible. In his words, he was going to hedge up her way with thorns.

Around the end of Hosea 2:11, though, the conversation mostly left Gomer and Hosea and went to God and Israel. And that is still the conversation taking place as we begin to examine this text.

A softening face

Hosea 2:14 *Therefore, behold, I will allure her, and bring her into the wilderness, and speak comfortably unto her.*

From verses nine through thirteen, God uttered some form of *I will* seven times. And all of them were negative; all of them spoke of judgment on Israel for what she had done. The *therefore* that begins verse fourteen is referring back to those seven terms of judgment. So the thought runs like this. "Therefore, because of all this judgment that I bring up on her, because of all the devastation she experienced at my hand, behold, I will allure her, and bring her into the wilderness, and speak comfortably unto her."

You see, God's judgments on His people are directed towards reconciliation rather than ruin. God had every right to simply leave this account at the point of judgment and destruction. But He did not.

There would come a point at which Hosea's efforts to make Gomer's life in sin miserable accomplished that goal. There would come a point at which God's efforts to make Israel's life in sin miserable accomplished that goal. There will come a point at which God's efforts to make your life in sin or my life in sin miserable accomplishes that goal.

But the God who extends the rod of judgment delights in extending the olive branch once the rod of judgment has done its work. And in verse fourteen, the hard and stern face of God has now softened toward Israel as He says *Therefore, behold, I will allure her, and bring her into the wilderness, and speak comfortably unto her.*

God was looking ahead to a time in the future when Israel, sick to death of her misery brought on by her sin, would be willing to heed the voice of God again. At that point, He determined to allure her, bring her into the wilderness, and speak comfortably to her. All three of these things are positive. Some commentators mistakenly view "bring her into the wilderness" as a negative among the positive, but that does not even begin to fit the context of this portion of the passage.

When He said that He would allure her, it is from the Hebrew word *pawthaw*, and it means, among other things, to persuade, to seduce, to entice. It is used here as a word of romance and intrigue. When we describe a person in our day as being alluring, that is the same picture being painted here. As Israel looked to the face of God once again, they would find a twinkle in His eyes and a smile on His face as He drew them back to Himself.

When He said that He would *bring her into the wilderness*, it is much the same picture as is painted in the romance book of the Bible, the Song of Solomon:

Song of Solomon 8:5 *Who is this that cometh up from the wilderness, leaning upon her beloved?*

The wilderness in these two passages was some private place apart from the crowd where a husband and wife could be alone. Adam Clark, though he seems to have missed or simply bypassed the romantic side of this, still came close to getting this one right, saying, "Instead of making her a public example, he takes her in private, talks to and reasons with her..." (Clarke, 627)

When He said that He would *speak comfortably unto her*, here is what you should know. It is from the word *leb,* and 508 times in the Bible when you see the word heart, this is the word that it comes from. He was basically saying, "I will talk to her heart to heart."

He could have merely spoken factually to her, but at this point, He would to speak comfortably to her instead.

Hosea 2:15 *And I will give her her vineyards from thence, and the valley of Achor for a door of hope: and she shall sing there, as in the days of her youth, and as in the day when she came up out of the land of Egypt.*

Back in verse five, Gomer had determined to pursue her lovers based on the list of things they were wont to give her. That list was as follows: bread, water, wool, flax, oil, and drink. Hosea, though, had given her corn and wine and oil, vast quantities of silver and gold, and also wool and flax.

Here, God far surpasses even all of that, determining to give Israel vineyards from the wilderness and the entire valley of Achor as a door of hope.

One of the things that God mentioned to Israel repeatedly as they made their way to Canaan was that it was a land of vineyards and that He would simply give it to them as such. Joshua reminded them of that when they arrived:

Joshua 24:13 *And I have given you a land for which ye did not labour, and cities which ye built not, and ye dwell in them; of the vineyards and oliveyards which ye planted not do ye eat.*

Israel was going to lose that land, being taken away from it into captivity. But there would come a day when she would be right with God and would be brought back to that land of vineyards.

As for God giving them the valley of Achor as a door of hope, there was both a play on words and a nod to a dark spot in their past being referenced.

The dark spot in their past is where the Valley of Achor actually got its name. It refers back to Joshua 7 and the events that transpired after the battle of Jericho up to the battle of Ai. A man named Achan secretly took some things he was not supposed to take from the overthrow of Jericho, and Israel lost the next battle, Ai, as a result. Thirty-six men lost their lives. Husbands and fathers and brothers did not make it home to their wives and children and siblings because of the sin of Achan.

When all was made known, Achan and his family were stoned to death and burned by fire, and a heap of stones was piled on the remains of their bodies as a memorial of what happened. That valley on that day was renamed the Valley of Achor. Achor means trouble; the Valley of Achor was the Valley of Trouble.

The play on words, then, was the fact that God was going to give repentant Israel their Valley of Trouble back to them as a Door of Hope. This place that had marked her first disobedience in the land, her first disaster, her first experience of God bringing disaster upon them for their rebellion, went on to become the doorway through which they marched into the rest of the land and gained all that God had for them.

It seems very much that when they returned bit by bit from captivity, they likely came through this very door of hope. It seems even more likely that when they make a wholesale return in the latter days, they will do so yet again. And when happens, the rest of the verse tells us *and she shall sing there, as in the days of her youth, and as in the day when she came up out of the land of Egypt.*

In Exodus 15:1-21, right after God delivered the children of Israel at the Red Sea, they sang. They were now two million people in the wilderness facing a thousand unknowns, and yet they took time to sing a song thanking God for what He had done. God refers to that here in this verse of Hosea, and says that the children of Israel would do the same thing when God brings them back.

Singing is a most appropriate and natural way for God's children to express their thanks to Him; heaven will forever be full of it (Revelation 5:9, 14:3, 15:3), and earth should be as well.

A sweet forgetfulness

Hosea 2:16 *And it shall be at that day, saith the LORD, that thou shalt call me Ishi; and shalt call me no more Baali.*

There is an amazing tenderness in this verse, and also something so relatable that it should bring a smile to our faces. Jehovah God told Israel that once they were finally reconciled to him, that day they would call Him *Ishi* rather than *Baali*. And these words fit perfectly well into the personal relationship of Hosea and Gomer as well, and were doubtless true for them.

So, what in the world are these *Ishi* and *Baali* names that God referenced in this place?

Let's start with *Ishi*. The first place it is found in Scripture is in the early chapters of Genesis.

God begins to mention the word man in Genesis 1:26. And in that place, He uses the pretty familiar word *adahm*—Adam:

Genesis 1:26 *And God said, Let us make* **man** *[Adahm] in our image, after our likeness...*

It is the same word in Genesis 1:27, 2:5, 2:7, 2:8, 2:15, 2:16, 2:18, and 2:22. Eleven uses of the word man in nine verses, and all eleven are from *Adahm.*

But in Genesis 2:22, Adam wakes up from the surgery God has just performed on him, and God is bringing him the lovely product of that surgery – Eve. And when Adam saw her, he decided to use a new word for man:

Genesis 2:23 *And Adam said, This is now bone of my bones, and flesh of my flesh: she shall be called Woman* [iysha], *because she was taken out of Man* [iysh].

This is where *ishi* came from. It literally means "my man!" It is what is spoken by a woman about her husband. Ma'am, your husband is your *Ishi*, he is "your man," your husband.

And this is what God said Israel would one day refer to Him as instead of Baali. You see, *Baali* means my Lord or my master. And while it is certainly true that God was and is Israel's Lord and Master, and was and is our Lord and Master, that is not where He wants the relationship day by day to settle. If it has to be a case where He has to continue to exercise His mastery of us and lordship over us by judging and chastising us until we get right, He will. But He would clearly much rather us simply do right because we love Him and enjoy being with Him.

In the relationship between Hosea and Gomer, the same picture was true. While he did have authority over her as the husband, something that Ephesians 5 makes clear is still for marriages today, that is not where he wanted the relationship day by day to settle. He would clearly much rather her simply do right because she loved him and wanted to be with him.

Another aspect of this, though, was the degradation of a word through time and circumstance. Again, *Baali* simply meant my Lord or my master, and there is nothing wrong with that at all. But because that word had been taken and for so long applied to the idols all around them—Baal, Baalzebub, Baalzephon, Baalim—God determined to remove it from their vocabulary.

Look at how serious He was about this:

Hosea 2:17 *For I will take away the names of Baalim out of her mouth, and they shall no more be remembered by their name.*

Because a good word had been corrupted by bad usage, God was going to take that word out of Israel's vocabulary to such a degree that the Baals would one day no more even be remembered by their name.

There is something so amazingly practical about that, and there is much we can still learn from it today. In our own language, there are many words that started off as good and practical and useful words that have for a very long time now been taken and twisted and corrupted to the point that they now mean something very different and very dirty. And if I so desired, I could list some of those words for you and do a very good job of defending their original meaning and their proper literary usage.

But I will never, ever do so. Because the moment I did, people would be horrified or hurt or angry or emboldened to go out and say those words to others who would be horrified or hurt or angry.

So I never say them, and I never write them. I don't need to; there are plenty of other non-corrupted words that I can still use to convey whatever truth needs to be conveyed without foolishly and needlessly doing harm.

Hosea 2:18 *And in that day will I make a covenant for them with the beasts of the field, and with the fowls of heaven, and with the creeping things of the ground: and I will break the bow and the sword and the battle out of the earth, and will make them to lie down safely.*

Israel was right then in their land and in prosperity but in sinfulness. Hosea was breaking the unwanted news that God was going to judge them for their sinfulness and would send them away into captivity in Assyria. They were going to hear the noise of war and battle. Their land was going to be wrecked and ruined and ravaged by wild animals in their diminishment.

But now, God was moving ahead on the calendar—far ahead—to a time when neither nature nor man would cause them any angst. This verse describes the Millennial Reign of Christ, the one thousand-year period of time when Christ will rule all nations with a rod of iron and the curse on nature will be removed.

God is going to make things so good for them that they will forget all the bad.

A secure future

Hosea 2:19 *And I will betroth thee unto me for ever; yea, I will betroth thee unto me in righteousness, and in judgment, and in lovingkindness, and in mercies.* **20** *I will even betroth thee unto me in faithfulness: and thou shalt know the LORD.*

Three times in these two verses, God promises to betroth Israel to Himself. The betrothal was a marriage covenant. This was far more than our Western version of an engagement. When people were betrothed, as is famously well-known from the case of Mary and Joseph, it took a divorce to break that union, just as if the marriage ceremony had already taken place.

There is something very notable and relevant to theological discourse today in this passage. God told Israel that He was going to be married to her—three times He said it here—and that it would be "forever" (v.19).

This is yet another passage in Scripture that exposes Replacement Theology as the mindless drivel that it truly is. For those who do not know, Replacement Theology is the teaching that Israel has been forever set aside and replaced by the church, and all of the promises that would have gone to her now come to us.

And all that is necessary for that to be true is for God to be a complete liar.

Which He isn't.

God said in these verses that He would betroth Israel to Himself in righteousness, judgment, lovingkindness, mercies, and faithfulness. Once again, Adam Clark does a fine job summarizing what is being said:

> "In righteousness: According to law, reason, and equity.
>
> In judgment: According to what is fit and becoming.
>
> In lovingkindness: Having the utmost affection and love for thee.
>
> In mercies: Forgiving and blotting out all past miscarriages.
>
> In faithfulness: Thou shalt no more prostitute thyself to idols, but be faithful to him who calls himself thy husband." (Clarke, 627)

All of this shows both the unchanging nature of God and the changed nature of Israel. God has determined to do a work in her that ends up with their permanent unification, and He will do so. And the result of this, according to the end of verse twenty will be *and thou shalt know the LORD.*

The reason Israel was going through what they were going through to begin with is that they did not really know the LORD. If they had really known Him, their behavior would have demonstrated it.

The reason many churchgoing people today go through what they go through is that they do not really know the LORD. If they did really know Him, their behavior would demonstrate it.

Hosea 2:21 *And it shall come to pass in that day, I will hear, saith the LORD, I will hear the heavens, and they shall hear the earth;* **22** *And the earth shall hear the corn, and the wine, and the oil; and they shall hear Jezreel.*

Throughout the Old Testament and God's dealings with Israel, a repeated refrain was that they would sin, fall under judgment, and then complain that it seemed that God did not hear their prayer. And there was a reason for that:

1 Samuel 8:18 *And ye shall cry out in that day because of your king which ye shall have chosen you; and the LORD will not hear you in that day.*

Psalm 66:18 *If I regard iniquity in my heart, the Lord will not hear me:*

Isaiah 1:15 And *when ye spread forth your hands, I will hide mine eyes from you: yea, when ye make many prayers, I will not hear: your hands are full of blood.*

But speaking of the days to come when Israel would repent of her sin and truly seek after God, God had Hosea write these words:

Hosea 2:21 *And it shall come to pass in that day, I will* **hear***, saith the LORD, I will* **hear** *the heavens, and they shall* **hear** *the earth;* **22** *And the earth shall* **hear** *the corn, and the wine, and the oil; and they shall* **hear** *Jezreel.*

During the Millennial Reign of Christ, everyone and everything will hear. God started by saying that He Himself would hear, would intentionally listen. He said that He would hear the heavens, and they, the heavens, would hear the earth, and the earth would hear the corn and wine and oil which was growing and flowing, and they, the corn and the wine and the oil would hear Jezreel, meaning the people who had been scattered abroad and now had returned to their land.

Hosea 2:23 *And I will sow her unto me in the earth; and I will have mercy upon her that had not obtained mercy; and I* *will say to them which were not my people, Thou art my people; and they shall say, Thou art my God.*

Verse twenty-two ended with the name Jezreel. As I have been pointing out throughout this study, it means to scatter, to sow as one would sow seeds. As it has been used in reference to God's judgment on Israel, though, this sowing has been to the four winds and to the corners of the earth. Rather than carefully placing the seed in a fertile field there in the land, God has scattered it, them, from the land.

I point that out because of how verse twenty-three starts. The beginning words are *And I will sow her unto me in the earth.* This is a bit of a lovely play on the meaning of words. God could have used the word for Jezreel to describe His restoration of Israel, but since He had already used that word to describe His scattering of Israel, He instead used the word *zara*.

Both indicate a sowing, a scattering. But by using a new word, He introduces a new sowing, saying *I will sow her unto me in the earth*. He would sow her abroad to others across the earth, but when she repented, he would turn and sow her to Himself in the earth. And once again, this defies the senseless spoutings of Replacement Theology.

As God closes out this chapter, He brings things full circle to where we started in chapter one:

...and I will have mercy upon her that had not obtained mercy; and I will say to them which were not my people, Thou art my people; and they shall say, Thou art my God.

This goes right back to the names of two of the children that Hosea and Gomer had together. Loruhama meant no more mercy. Loammi meant not my people. That is how things were going to start for Israel as God brought this round of judgment to them. But it will all change forever in the day when God drops both of the prefixes and once again calls Israel by Ruhama and Ammi, and they say to Him, "Thou art my God."

A door of hope. No one ever needs that kind of thing more than children of God who have sinned and then been scattered by God. And for those who are willing to truly repent, for those who are desirous of having that tender *ishi* relationship with God where they truly love Him with all of their hearts and want nothing more than to please Him in all things, that doorway will always be available.

I highly recommend it.

Chapter Five
Love When It Matters Most

Hosea 3:1 *Then said the LORD unto me, Go yet, love a woman beloved of her friend, yet an adulteress, according to the love of the LORD toward the children of Israel, who look to other gods, and love flagons of wine.* **2** *So I bought her to me for fifteen pieces of silver, and for an homer of barley, and an half homer of barley:* **3** *And I said unto her, Thou shalt abide for me many days; thou shalt not play the harlot, and thou shalt not be for another man: so will I also be for thee.* **4** *For the children of Israel shall abide many days without a king, and without a prince, and without a sacrifice, and without an image, and without an ephod, and without teraphim:* **5** *Afterward shall the children of Israel return, and seek the LORD their God, and David their king; and shall fear the LORD and his goodness in the latter days.*

In the last section of verses, Gomer was gone, and Hosea was explaining to the children that he intended to make her life in sin as difficult as possible so that she would remember how good she had it when she was doing right. He then explained that when she finally got to the point of brokenness and desperation, he would take her back and treat her as wonderfully as if she never left.

But in real life, everyone knows that kind of a thing is much easier said than done. The bitterness tends to build on itself with each new day of abandonment, and there usually comes a point at which the abandoned spouse wants only the worst for the one who left – so much so that they often even rejoice when it finally happens, rather than restoring them as they had originally intended.

For Hosea, there did indeed come a day when he would have to make that call.

A supernatural decree

Hosea 3:1 *Then said the LORD unto me, Go yet, love a woman beloved of her friend, yet an adulteress, according to the love of the LORD toward the children of Israel, who look to other gods, and love flagons of wine.*

Hosea 3 brings us to a truly remarkable point in time in Scripture. This is the point at which God had a conversation with Hosea from the perspective of one jilted husband speaking to another jilted husband. Hosea had taken Gomer in when she was utterly unworthy, had loved her unconditionally, and yet had been abandoned. God had taken Israel in when she was utterly unworthy, had loved her unconditionally, and yet had been abandoned.

And that is the perspective being expressed by God in this first verse of chapter three.

There is no way to know how long Gomer was away or how deep the despair and hopelessness in Hosea's heart got. But there came a day in which God spoke to Hosea once again. The same God who spoke to him initially and told him to go take this woman to wife now came to him and told him that it was time to go take her in that same capacity yet again.

The words He opened the conversation with were, "*Go yet, love a woman beloved of her friend, yet an adulteress.*"

Let's compare this to the first time God commanded Hosea to take Gomer, because there is a subtle difference well worth noticing:

Hosea 1:2 *...Go, take unto thee a wife of whoredoms and children of whoredoms...*

The first time, God said *Go...*

The second time, He said *Go yet...*

And it is not at all difficult to understand both the difference and the why. *Go yet* was God's way of saying something like "Go again. Go in spite of what has happened. Go even though your flesh and emotions may not feel like going. Go even though you might rather sit back and revel in her fall. Go yet..."

God told him to *Go yet, love a woman beloved of her friend, yet an adulteress*. The woman beloved of her friend was Gomer. The friend who still loved her was Hosea. And yet, she was an adulteress – Hosea knew it, and God acknowledged it. Nothing good is ever served from sweeping sin under the rug and acting as if it did not and does not exist. If we are to love like God, we will love in spite of the sin while never minimizing the sin for so much as a moment. And in fact, loving like God was the point of all of this, because the last half of the verse says *according to the love of the LORD toward the children of Israel, who look to other gods, and love flagons of wine.*

Hosea was to go love Gomer according to, or in like manner as the love of the LORD toward the children of Israel. And this matches the teaching of the New Testament as well:

Ephesians 5:25 *Husbands, love your wives, <u>even as Christ also loved the church</u>, and gave himself for it;*

When we love as we love, we will not love anywhere near enough. When we love as Christ loves, we will never fail to love enough.

Yes, Gomer committed adultery against Hosea. Yes, Israel looked to other gods and loved flagons of wine. Gomer was an immoral wife. Israel was a drunken and idolatrous nation. Both had cheated on the ones who loved them when they were unworthy. Both would experience a loving and merciful supernatural decree beginning with Go yet...

A shocking display

Hosea 3:2 *So I bought her to me for fifteen pieces of silver, and for an homer of barley, and an half homer of barley:*

I want you to understand as you read this verse that Hosea himself wrote it, which means that this was a current event, and therefore something that everyone knew about. As the prophet of God and one who had already entered into a scandalous marriage with Gomer, everyone was watching and was aware of what was going on in their relationship. I mention that because, given what this verse means, we would expect it to be an entire chapter or two, and we would expect it to be given in much greater detail. And the reason that is not the case is simply because everyone in Hosea's day knew about it, and therefore it was not necessary for him to describe it.

Quite simply, this verse lets us know that Hosea's wife, Gomer, got so low that she ended up being sold as a slave. Look at what Moses wrote nearly a thousand years before this time:

Exodus 21:32 *If the ox shall push a manservant or a maidservant; he shall give unto their master thirty shekels of silver, and the ox shall be stoned.*

Starting back in verse twenty-eight of Exodus 21, we find that the context of this is the death of a person by being gored by an ox. And in that context, in verse thirty-two, many generations before Hosea, we find the life of a slave valued at thirty shekels of silver. Mind you, this was top price for a slave that had died. When buying a slave, no one had to bid that much, nor would anyone bid that much if a slave was not fit. But this was just the customary rate that was expected, and that law never changed, even up into Hosea's day and beyond. And that purchase price is what locks in for us the fact that we are dealing with Hosea buying Gomer back as a slave, not giving a dowry to parents or a price to some lover.

So fast forward to Hosea's day when Gomer finds herself up for auction. The price that won the bidding for her was fifteen pieces of silver and a homer and a half of barley, which amounted to fifteen ephahs of barley, something along the lines of fifteen bushels. An ephah of barley in those days was worth one shekel of silver.(Keil, 68) So Hosea was able to pay the standard thirty shekel price of a slave, half in silver and half in barley grain, which was the roughest and least desirable of grains in those days, and usually reserved for livestock. Gomer had indeed gotten very low.

All of that, though, is merely the sterile facts and figures of the financial transaction. There is much more to what happened on that day and in this verse, especially when you consider that a flesh and blood human being was at the center of it all.

By way of background, understand that slavery itself has been around for nearly as long as humanity itself has existed. And most every race has both been enslaved and been the enslaver of others at various times. The very word slave comes from the German word *sklave*, indicating a person of the Slavonic race who had been enslaved: Russians, Ukrainians, Belarusians, Poles, Czechs, Slovaks, and others. (ISBE, 2815)

There are some things we can piece together about slaves and their sale both from Scripture and from historical accounts of the ancient world. It is widely known that slaves were often displayed and then sold naked – they were regarded as goods, and that allowed people to see what they were buying. And during the time period in question as we study Hosea, when they were so far from God, there is a biblical indication that that was then the case with them as well. During the time period of the divided kingdom, there was a battle between Israel and Judah that resulted in a victory for Israel and many captives being taken from Judah to Samaria, the capital of Israel. Notice what is said in that account:

2 Chronicles 28:10 *And now ye purpose to keep under the children of Judah and Jerusalem for bondmen and bondwomen unto you: but are there not with you, even with you, sins against the LORD your God?*

So the purpose for them taking these captives was to use them and trade them and sell them as slaves. With that understanding, drop down a few more verses. A prophet has chewed them out, and they are now going to try and make things right:

2 Chronicles 28:14 *So the armed men left the captives and the spoil before the princes and all the congregation.* **15** *And the men which were expressed by name rose up, and took the captives, and with the spoil* **clothed all that were naked among them,** *and arrayed them, and shod them, and gave them to eat and to drink, and anointed them, and carried all the feeble of them upon asses, and brought them to Jericho, the city of palm trees, to their brethren: then they returned to Samaria.*

They were going to be sold as slaves, so they had stripped them for that purpose.

With that understanding, let's go back to the slave market on that day when Gomer was being sold. We know from all that we have studied thus far that she had been, for much of her life, an attractive and desirable individual. So much so that many different men sought her out to purchase her services for the night. So much so that she was confident, even after several years of marriage, that she would have no trouble reestablishing her lucrative business once she abandoned the home.

But the thing about a life of sin is that it wears on people in every way possible.

When I was a young boy, there were two girls just a couple of years older than me that were both some of the most beautiful things you would ever see. In school, every boy fought for their attention. Either one could legitimately have been a model.

They went very different ways in life. One married her high school sweetheart and is with him to this day, and their whole family has been in church serving the Lord the entire way. The other was wildly promiscuous, drank, smoke, and dabbled in drugs.

I went about thirty-five years without seeing either of them and then saw both of them within a few months of each other. The first one very legitimately looked just as beautiful and fit and healthy now as she did thirty-five years ago; she looked like she had hardly aged a day.

The second one looked like she had spent her life living under a bridge somewhere. She looked old and used up. She was missing most of her teeth. She was a wreck, and she looked nothing like she once did; I almost did not believe it was her when we were reintroduced.

This is what a life of sin does to people, and Gomer found that out the hard way.

There came a day when she was no longer attractive. There came a day when not only did none of her lovers want her for a wife, they did not even want her for a one-night stand. There came a day when she could not afford to feed herself or pay any of her bills. There came a day when she found herself in debt to her creditors with no way to pay.

And then there came a day when she found herself in the public square, having to take her clothes off in the light of day rather than in the intimacy of the night.

She was broken. She had left her husband, her children were with him, her lovers did not want her, and strange men were leering at her, trying to decide if she was even worth bidding on for any purpose.

Oh, the scene that must have played out on that day!

"Ladies and gentlemen, we have here one female slave for sale. She clearly isn't worth much, but surely someone can find some use for her!"

Laughter wafts across the crowd, lurid, dirty laughter. Jokes pass back and forth about the used-up woman that so many of them knew very well but did not really know at all.

"I'll start the bidding at five shekels," comes a voice from the front. "Maybe she can at least dance a bit while she mops the floor for me."

More laughter, as tears begin to well up in Gomer's eyes. She does not want to let them flow; this is humiliating enough. So she swallows hard and turns her head a bit, closing her eyes.

"Turn in a circle, woman," comes another voice, the voice of a man that everyone knows to be cruel and violent. "Let's see what we are dealing with."

Gomer stands still, unwilling to obey. But a slap across the face from the auctioneer changes her mind and brings laughter from the crowd as she slowly turns about.

"Good, good," comes the sickening voice. "I'll bid seven shekels. I have plans for this one."

Gomer drops her head and begins to cry.

"Ten" comes a voice from the back.

Gomer chokes back the tears and begins to tremble. Everyone turns to hear the new voice, a voice that she knows without even having to look.

"Well, if it isn't Hosea, the prophet – or should I say, the HUSBAND!" the auctioneer roars. The crowd joins him in laughter, delighted at such an unexpected and intriguing turn of events.

Hosea does not flinch; his bid is placed, and he is not reacting to the crowd. His eyes are on his wife – a wife whose head is still bowed.

"Twelve!" comes another voice. "Suddenly, this woman is interesting to me!"

More laughter, as all eyes turn back to Hosea. How far will he take this?

"Fifteen pieces of silver," he says firmly.

"Fifteen pieces of silver and a homer of barley," his competition shouts in response. The crowd gasps; she is no longer worth anywhere near that by this point; the man is just bidding things up because of Hosea. And surely this will be it; there is no way Hosea will actually pay full price for this woman who has wrecked their home and now is just a shadow of her former self.

"Fifteen pieces of silver and a homer and a half of barley," Hosea calmly replies.

Another gasp from the crowd. They cannot believe what they are hearing. When the auction began, everyone wondered if anyone would buy this woman; no one would have ever dreamed that someone would pay full price for her. And from the look on Hosea's face, it is clear that if necessary he will do much more than this; he will give everything he owns to bring this woman home.

"I have fifteen shekels of silver and a homer and a half of barley; thirty shekels of silver worth of a bid. Do I hear thirty-five? Thirty-five, going once, going twice... sold at fifteen shekels of silver and a homer and a half of barley! Congratulations, sir, you may come pay for your... property."

Gomer bursts into tears. She is honestly not sure what is going to happen now; she just knows she wants to get off of that stage.

Hosea quickly hands the auctioneer the silver and arranges for the delivery of the barley. Then he makes his way to his bride, slips a robe around her to cover her shame, and pulls her into his chest to hold her while she completely breaks and sobs uncontrollably.

I rather suspect that he picked her up and carried her home in his arms that day.

A sweet determination

I am so grateful that God allowed there to be a day when Hosea would put pen to parchment and actually write out the words he said to Gomer after he purchased her. We have those exact words in verse three:

Hosea 3:3 *And I said unto her, Thou shalt abide for me many days; thou shalt not play the harlot, and thou shalt not be for another man: so will I also be for thee.*

I do not know when Hosea said these words to his wife, but I would be willing to bet most everything that I own that he said them to her as he took her home that day.

These words are not Hallmark words. These words are not "And they immediately kissed and made up and lived happily ever after." Yes, Hosea was taking her home, but there was work yet to be done.

In verse one, God specifically told Hosea to go and **love** Gomer again. You really need to understand that in light of what is said here. Gomer told Hosea *Thou shalt abide for me many days*. That word for abide means to wait. Gomer was going to have to wait for Hosea for a good while. What in the world does that mean in light of the fact that God told him to love her, and that he said in verse two that he "bought her **to** me"?

What it means is that he took her home that day, but rather than just hopping into bed, they went through a lengthy time period, "many days," where they did not behave in that way as man and wife. They were married, yes, but they basically started over in their courtship even while they lived under the same roof as man and wife. They almost certainly stayed in different rooms for a good while. All of her needs were met, and she was getting stronger and healthier by the day. But Hosea was going to make sure that she did not simply recover and then bolt again before he reestablished conjugal relations with her. They were not going to be intimate until he was absolutely certain that the change in her was for real this time.

Here were the conditions he established for them both during this probationary period at the end of this verse:

Thou shalt not play the harlot, and thou shalt not be for another man: so will I also be for thee.

We do not know how long those many days lasted. But we do know that Hosea's terms were that during that time, she would be absolutely faithful to him, and he would be absolutely faithful to her. There would not be sex, but there would be love and affection and fidelity.

You say, "That doesn't sound so sweet to me."

I say that if you really consider it, it is just about the sweetest thing ever.

Hosea clearly desired what every man desires. And under the law of Moses, he had every legal and moral right to put her away forever and then marry whoever he would and enjoy the marriage bed every single day. Instead, he met her needs and rebuilt the broken bonds with her – bonds that she broke—while expecting nothing in return other than her faithfulness. In other words, she was finally going to see what she never could seem to grasp before, namely that he was not like other men.

A statement of destiny

The odd-sounding arrangement of verse three had a point in the mind and heart and plan of God. And here was that point:

Hosea 3:4 *For the children of Israel shall abide many days without a king, and without a prince, and without a sacrifice, and without an image, and without an ephod, and without teraphim:* **5** *Afterward shall the children of Israel return, and seek the LORD their God, and David their king; and shall fear the LORD and his goodness in the latter days.*

The word *for* that begins this one sentence of two verses ties everything in these two verses back to Hosea's arrangement in verse three, and the many days of verse four is a parallel to the many days of verse three. It was a picture of what was to come between God and Israel.

It begins in verse four with God letting Israel know that they were going to be without six particular things for a very long period of time. Those six things were a king, a prince, a sacrifice, an image, an ephod, and a teraphim.

There is much to see there.

Israel finally fell to Assyria in 2 Kings 18:10, in 722 B.C. Hoshea was on the throne – and he was the last actual king of the nation of Israel. They have had neither king nor prince since that day, more than 2,700 years worth of "many days."

They have also been without a sacrifice for a very long period of many days, and this refers to the prescribed sacrifices to Jehovah as specified in the Mosaic law. They had already given all of that up anyway in favor of their golden calf worship and Baal worship. But now they would find themselves in a situation where they could not have that sacrifice even if they would. They were carried far away from the neighboring Southern Kingdom of Judah, where the Temple still stood, and such sacrifices were still offered. That Temple would then fall 136 years later when Nebuchadnezzar sacked Jerusalem. It would be rebuilt for the Southern Kingdom once they returned, and then Herod's Temple would replace it a bit over five hundred years later. And then that Temple would be destroyed in the siege of Jerusalem in A.D. 70. The Ark of the Covenant was gone long before that, though. So in truth, they have been without a sacrifice for even longer than they have currently been without a king.

An image is the next thing that they would be without for many days. Image is from the word *mahtseba*, and it means pillar or memorial. It was an object of idolatrous worship. So God was not only going to remove from them the ability to worship Him as they once had, He was even going to remove their ability to worship their idols as well.

Keil and Delitzsch put it this way:

"With the removal of the monarchy, or the dissolution of the kingdom, not only was the Jehovah worship abolished, but an end was also put the idolatry of the nation, since the people discover the worthlessness of the idols from the fact that, when the judgment burst upon them, they could grant no deliverance; and notwithstanding the circumstance that, when carried into exile, they were transported in the midst of idolaters, the distress and misery into which they were then plunged filled them abhorrence of idolatry." (Keil, 71)

They would also be without an ephod for many days. We first read of the ephod in Exodus 25. The ephod was worn by the high priest over the tunic and robe. It consisted of two finely wrought pieces which hung down, the one in front over the breast, the other on the back, to the middle of the thigh; joined on the shoulders by golden clasps set in onyx stones with the names of the twelve tribes, and fastened round the waist by a girdle. (Jamieson, 468) The urim and thummim, the apparatus by which God often made his will known to them, belonged to the breastplate, which was attached to the ephod. (Clarke, 630)

All of this tells us that for many days, Israel would be without a priest who was actually sanctioned by God and could speak authoritatively to the people from God.

They had abandoned the priesthood years ago in favor of their own idolatrous priests. The real priesthood would continue on without them for a bit longer, and then would exist only in fits and starts for a while, and then would be done away with entirely when the Temple in Jerusalem finally fell.

Finally, they would be without a teraphim. And if you are not quite certain what that is, that is likely because it is so very rarely mentioned in Scripture and was not part of the Mosaic law or the worship of Jehovah at all. Teraphim is only mentioned in two instances in the Bible, here, and in Judges 17 and 18 in another reference to idolatry. A teraphim was a household idol. So can we find that in their fall, they would not only lose the true religion that was their birthright but even the false religion that was ever their bane. They would become functional atheists. And even now in our day, that is in large measure what many of them are. They give lip service to some God somewhere, but in the day-by-day reality of their life, there is none.

But God said "many days," not forever.

Hosea 3:5 *Afterward shall the children of Israel return, and seek the LORD their God, and David their king; and shall fear the LORD and his goodness in the latter days.*

A truly beautiful word starts this verse, the word *afterward*. It is an indication that one day, Gomer's heart would finally be changed to such a degree that she would seek after her husband with all of it. It is an indication that one day, Israel's heart would finally be changed to such a degree that she would seek after her God with all of it.

Something unique is said in this verse that should compel our attention: *Afterward shall the children of Israel return, and seek the LORD their God, and David their king.*

It is not surprising in the least to hear God say that the children of Israel would return and seek the LORD, Jehovah, their God. And they will. They have not truly sought Him as a people for 2,700 years or more, but they will. But it is surprising to read that they will seek David their king. The question we need to ask about this is whether this somehow refers to the David that had already been dead for hundreds of years by the time of Hosea and Gomer, or if it means something else.

The most common opinion on this subject is that it refers to the Messiah, Jesus, who came from the line of David. Many, though, hold the opinion that it refers to David himself who will be resurrected and once again serve as king. And the answer to which of these two things is correct is as follows:

Both.

Take a look at this:

Jeremiah 30:7 *Alas! for that day is great, so that none is like it: it is even the time of Jacob's trouble; but he shall be saved out of it.* **8** *For it shall come to pass in that day, saith the LORD of hosts, that I will break his yoke from off thy neck, and will burst thy bonds, and strangers shall no more serve themselves of him:* **9** *But they shall serve the LORD their God, and David their king, whom I will raise up unto them.*

God was pretty specific that they would both serve the LORD and David their king, and that this would come to pass after the time of Jacob's Trouble, meaning after the last half of the Tribulation Period. This, then, is the Millennial Reign of Christ that is spoken of. David will be one of many national kings and lower rulers under Christ during that time:

Revelation 20:4 *And I saw thrones, and they sat upon them, and judgment was given unto them: and I saw the souls of them that were beheaded for the witness of Jesus, and for the word of God, and which had not worshipped the beast, neither his image, neither had received his mark upon their foreheads,* *or in their hands; and <u>they lived and reigned with Christ a thousand years</u>.*

Israel had, by this point in her history, forsaken the line of David for several hundred years in favor of her own line of kings, starting with Jeroboam I. But there will come a day when all of the twelve tribes are reunited as one nation under David, their king, under Christ, his King, our King, everyone's King.

The very last phrase of this verse and chapter says, *and shall fear the LORD and his goodness in the latter days.*

That phrase "latter days" goes right back to what I just pointed out about the Tribulation Period and the Millennial Reign of Christ. In those days, Israel will fear both the Lord and His goodness.

That sounds a bit unusual, doesn't it? It seems like it would say that they would fear the Lord and appreciate His goodness, but instead, it says that they will fear both. How exactly does that work?

Among other things, this word for fear, *pahkad*, means to revere and to stand in awe of. For a very, very long time, Israel took both God and His goodness for granted. But there will come a day that He rescues and redeems them in such a dramatic fashion that only He could do, that they never take Him for granted again. It will not just be His judgment that makes them tremble but also His goodness.

Please remember, though, that we have all of this information and all of these promises and prophecies because of a very real husband who, just like Christ would later do for us, went and paid the full price to rescue his very real wife from the dire predicament she had gotten herself into. This was not just love; it was love when it mattered most.

Chapter Six
I Have a Bone to Pick With You

Hosea 4:1 *Hear the word of the LORD, ye children of Israel: for the LORD hath a controversy with the inhabitants of the land, because there is no truth, nor mercy, nor knowledge of God in the land.* **2** *By swearing, and lying, and killing, and stealing, and committing adultery, they break out, and blood toucheth blood.* **3** *Therefore shall the land mourn, and every one that dwelleth therein shall languish, with the beasts of the field, and with the fowls of heaven; yea, the fishes of the sea also shall be taken away.* **4** *Yet let no man strive, nor reprove another: for thy people are as they that strive with the priest.* **5** *Therefore shalt thou fall in the day, and the prophet also shall fall with thee in the night, and I will destroy thy mother.* **6** *My people are destroyed for lack of knowledge: because thou hast rejected knowledge, I will also reject thee, that thou shalt be no priest to me: seeing thou hast forgotten the law of thy God, I will also forget thy children.* **7** *As they were increased, so they sinned against me: therefore will I change their glory into shame.* **8** *They eat up the sin of my people, and they set their heart on their iniquity.* **9** *And there shall be, like people, like priest: and I will punish them for their ways, and reward them their doings.* **10** *For they shall eat, and not have enough: they shall commit whoredom, and shall not increase: because they have left off to* *take heed to the LORD.* **11** *Whoredom and wine and new wine take away the heart.*

The story of Hosea and Gomer is now complete. God does not tell us anything else about their lives together from this point on in the text. We are basically left with the seeming assurance from chapter three that they made it; their marriage survived and thrived. From this point on in the book of Hosea, everything will be about God and Israel, the very relationship that Hosea and Gomer became a living picture of.

A controversy

Hosea 4:1 *Hear the word of the LORD, ye children of Israel: for the LORD hath a controversy with the inhabitants of the land, because there is no truth, nor mercy, nor knowledge of God in the land.*

As Hosea begins to expound to Israel where they stand with God, he tells them to hear the word of the LORD because the LORD has a controversy with them. And when he tells them that, right after calling them the children of Israel, he calls them the inhabitants of the land. And if we are not careful, we will regard that as a mere redundancy when, in fact, there is a point to him using both monikers concerning them.

Yes, they were the children of Israel, descended from Abraham. But those children of Israel were inhabiting a very particular land that God gave them—and were at risk of losing that land because of their behavior.

God told Hosea to tell those people that He had a controversy with them. Controversy is from the word *reeb,* and it means a quarrel, a dispute, and sometimes it even indicates a lawsuit. As we would put in our vernacular, God was telling them that He had a bone to pick with them.

The controversy, as stated at this point, was that Israel was lacking three very important things. God said that there was no truth, mercy, or knowledge of God in the land. So they were deceptive in their sayings, destructive in their surroundings, and deficient in their spirituality. And the results were pretty hard to miss:

Hosea 4:2 *By swearing, and lying, and killing, and stealing, and committing adultery, they break out, and blood toucheth blood.*

How they were living in verse two ties directly back to all they were lacking in verse one.

They lacked truth, and the result was swearing and lying. This word for swearing is *alah*, and it does not mean uttering curse words; it means false swearing, uttering oaths that are not true.

They lacked mercy, and the result was killing and stealing. People who have mercy for others do not take the lives of those others nor steal from those others.

They lacked the knowledge of God, and the result was adultery and other hidden sins, things that, under more spiritual conditions, they would have understood that God saw and would judge.

God said that by those things, that swearing, and lying, and killing, and stealing, and committing adultery, they *break out, and blood toucheth blood.* To break out means to burst through every restraint. The law could not stop them from their wickedness, their parents could not stop them from their wickedness, the priests and prophets could not stop them from their wickedness, their conscience could not stop them from their wickedness, they were utterly unrestrained. And when this verse ends with the phrase "and blood toucheth blood," it means that the acts of violence were so frequent, one immediately after the other immediately after the other, that this victim's blood was touching that victim's blood which was touching some other victim's blood. (Jamieson, 470)

Please remember that we are not dealing with a time period in which people were poor and merely trying to survive. This was during one of the most prosperous periods in Israel's history. These people were not doing any of this because they had to; they were doing it because they wanted to.

Hosea 4:3 *Therefore shall the land mourn, and every one that dwelleth therein shall languish, with the beasts of the field, and with the fowls of heaven; yea, the fishes of the sea also shall be taken away.*

I just reminded you that they were in one of the most prosperous eras in their history. And yet, because of their constant violence and bloodshed and wickedness of all sorts, God painted a picture in this verse of a very bleak future that was coming their way. He began by saying that the land would mourn, and everyone that dwelt in it would languish. God was going to wreck and devastate their fruitful and prosperous land, and their licentiousness was going to give way to languishing. That word means to droop and to be exhausted.

But it would not just be the land and the people. When the people of the land do wrong, and God begins to judge that land that those people dwell in, even nature itself suffers. God said that they would languish *with the beasts of the field, and with the fowls of heaven; yea, the fishes of the sea also shall be taken away.*

The cattle and the lambs and livestock were going to be malnourished and sickly and weak. The birds were going to stop their joyful singing. Even the fish of the sea were going to be part of this judgment; God said that they would be taken away.

Adam Clarke said of that:

> "Those immense shoals which at certain seasons frequent the coasts, which are caught in millions, and become a very useful home supply, and a branch of most profitable traffic, they shall be directed by the unseen influence of God to

avoid our coasts, as has frequently been the case with herrings, mackerel, pilchards, &c.; and so this source of supply and wealth has been shut up, because of the iniquities of the land." (Clarke, 631)

That is very eloquent. But please allow me to put in simpler and starker and perhaps more memorable terms. God was going to make sure that all the fish of the sea got the memo to avoid Israeli coasts. He was going to make fishing anywhere near there like throwing a net or a line and hook out onto a parking lot.

A command

Hosea 4:4 *Yet let no man strive, nor reprove another: for thy people are as they that strive with the priest.*

In three relatively short verses, God painted a dire picture of Israel's sin and the consequences that were to follow. But while we may well assume that what would follow would be a command to rebuke such sin so that man could repent, the exact opposite command is given. After speaking of the sin of the people and the judgment to come, God said, *"Yet let no man strive, nor reprove another."*

He was instructing that even if any of them had a mind to see things change, if any of them were inclined to take God's side in this and to strive against those who were living wickedly and to approve them for their wickedness, he should not do so.

That is a shocking command. Usually, the opposite command is given:

Isaiah 58:1 *Cry aloud, spare not, lift up thy voice like a trumpet, and shew my people their transgression, and the house of Jacob their sins.*

But here in Hosea, God basically gave the exact opposite command that He gave in Isaiah, telling the people not to cry aloud and not to show people their transgressions and their sins.

Why in the world would He do that? The answer is found in the last phrase of verse four: *for thy people* [the people of the nation of Israel] *are as they that strive with the priest.*

Early on in Israel's history as a nation, way back in Exodus and Leviticus, God established the priests as the authorities over the people. To argue with them was analogous to arguing with God.

Please understand that there were a lot of times when the priests were as wicked as the people themselves. In fact, it will not take us many more words in this text to get to the fact that even then, they were. But God was using arguing with the priests in this text with the idea of the priesthood in its ideal sense, with priests who themselves were obedient to God and hearing from God. In so many words, God in this verse was telling people that Israel was not going to listen to anybody who would tell them that they were doing wrong and that, therefore, it wasn't even worth trying to tell them.

When a person or people get like that, the only thing left is destruction. And that is where Israel was at.

A calamity

Hosea 4:5 *Therefore shalt thou fall in the day, and the prophet also shall fall with thee in the night, and I will destroy thy mother.*

The *therefore* that begins verse five ties back to the last phrase of verse four, *for thy people are as they that strive with the priest.* Because no one could tell them anything, God said that they would fall in the day and that the prophet would fall with them in the night.

To fall in the day was an indication of open ruin and shame. And the fact that they were still going to be falling in the night tells us that there would be no interludes of peace and safety when the judgment came. The prophet falling with them was an indication that either those prophets at best knew what the people were doing wrong and just would not say so, or at worst, were actually participating in that sin along with the people.

But God also said that he would destroy their mother.

There are three pretty evenly divided opinions on this. View number one is that it referred to literal mothers who would not be spared when the judgment fell. Neither them being the weaker vessel nor them being aged would stop them from being broken along with their younger and stronger sons.

View number two is that it refers to Jerusalem as their mother city.

View number three is that it refers to the nation as a whole.

And the answer to which is yes.

All three of those were going to be destroyed in the coming judgments: real mothers, Jerusalem, and Israel. Sin is like that, breaking things much farther and wider than people imagine when they start into that life of sin.

Hosea 4:6 *My people are destroyed for lack of knowledge: because thou hast rejected knowledge, I will also reject thee, that thou shalt be no priest to me: seeing thou hast forgotten the law of thy God, I will also forget thy children.*

The first phrase of verse six is often quoted in regard to preachers who will not preach and teach sound doctrine. And while that is certainly a travesty and is amply addressed elsewhere in Scripture, that is the exact opposite problem of the one God states here. He said specifically that they were destroyed for lack of knowledge because they rejected knowledge.

It was available. The knowledge of God and His righteous expectations for their behavior was available in written form and through prophets like Hosea. They had access to that knowledge; they just rejected it.

It is interesting that at the very outset of verse six, God speaks of the destruction of His people as having already happened. He said *My people are destroyed for lack of knowledge.* John Wesley observed that "Many were already cut off by Pul king of Assyria, and many destroyed by the bloody tyranny of Menahem." (Linder, John Wesley Notes) And yet, the ultimate judgment at the hand of the Assyrians was yet to come—and was just as certain to come as if it, like those other calamities, had already happened.

Now look again at the second phrase of the verse attached to what follows:

Because thou hast rejected knowledge, I will also reject thee, that thou shalt be no priest to me:

The judgment matched the sin; the effect matched the cause. Because the people rejected the knowledge of God, God was going to reject them. And He was specifically going to do so to the end that they would no longer be regarded as a priest to Him.

That last phrase bears a bit of explanation. Who was the priest that He was talking about?

Keil and Delitzsch get this one just right, saying that this was:

> "The whole nation of the ten tribes which adhered to the image worship set up by Jeroboam, with its illegal priesthood (1 Kings 12:26-33), in spite of all the divine threats and judgments, through which one dynasty after another was destroyed, and would not desist from this sin of Jeroboam. The Lord would therefore reject it from being priest, i.e. would deprive it of

the privilege of being a priestly nation (Exodus 19:6), would strip it of its priestly rank, and make it like the heathen." (Keil, 78)

Here is that verse from Exodus that they referenced:

Exodus 19:6 *And ye shall be unto me a kingdom of priests, and an holy nation. These are the words which thou shalt speak unto the children of Israel.*

God expected the whole world to be able to go to Israel as a people and hear from God, and know how to follow Him. That was a high station—and they threw it all away in their pursuit of iniquity and idolatry.

Here is how He ended verse six: *Seeing thou hast forgotten the law of thy God, I will also forget thy children.*

Their forgetfulness was not absent-mindedness; it was intentional. They chose to forget the law of God because they did not like it. It told them that a lot of the things they were doing were wrong and that they needed to stop.

God's forgetfulness was going to be equally intentional. And it was ultimately going to fall on their children. They brought their children up in iniquity and idolatry, those children loved it just as much as their parents, and many of those parents were one day going to die with their last earthly sight being that of their children being hauled away to Assyria.

Parents, before you choose a life of sin, you would do well to remember that your children normally have far more years to live with the consequences than you do.

Hosea 4:7 *As they were increased, so they sinned against me: therefore will I change their glory into shame.*

I have been pointing out to you all during this study that much of what we read in the book of Hosea was taking place during the prosperous time period in which Jeroboam II was on the throne. That is reflected here in verse seven when God uses the words "as they were increased." Numerically, financially, militarily, Israel was prospering and thriving during this time period. But as they were increased, all of which increase was a blessing from God, they increased their sin to match it. The better God was to them, the more disobedient they were to Him. And that brought a *therefore* that they did not want to hear. God said *therefore,* because the more I have blessed them the more they have sinned, *therefore will I change their glory into shame.* A blessed people who choose sin will become a blistered people for whom God chooses shame.

Hosea 4:8 *They eat up the sin of my people, and they set their heart on their iniquity.*

Verse eight begins a bit of a specific focus in this text, a focus that will go all the way through verse ten. God has been dealing with the sins of the nation as a whole; He will now focus that more particularly on the priesthood.

The phrase *They eat up the sin of my people* is clearly a pretty unique phrase, occurring only here in the entire Bible. So who is the *they*, and how is anyone eating up the sin of others?

Here is what you need to know. This word for sin is from the word *khat-ah-ah*, and it often refers simultaneously both to a sin and to the offering for sin. With that understanding, let me show you another place in Scripture where it is used along with a reference to eating:

Leviticus 6:25 *Speak unto Aaron and to his sons, saying, This is the law of the <u>sin offering</u>* [khat-ah-ah]*: In the place where the burnt offering is killed shall the <u>sin offering</u>* [khat-ah-ah] *be killed before the LORD: it is most holy.* **26** *The priest that offereth it for <u>sin</u>* [khat-ah] *shall* **eat** *it: in the holy place shall it be* **eaten***, in the court of the tabernacle of the congregation.*

When the people brought a lamb for a sin offering, part of it was burned before the Lord, but part of it was cooked and eaten by the priest and his families; it was literally how they put food on their tables. So for them to be eating the sin offering was, in a way, them eating the sin of others. Keep that in mind as we look at verse eight again, particularly focusing on the last phrase of it this time:

Hosea 4:8 *They eat up the sin of my people, and **they set their heart on their iniquity**.*

They, the priests, were setting their heart on the iniquity of the people. As Keil and Delitzsch put it, "They wished the sins of the people to be increased, in order that they might receive a good supply of sacrificial meat to eat." (Keil, 79)

Let that sink in. The priests of Israel were not hoping that people would live right and do right; they were hoping that the people would do more and more wickedness more and more regularly so that they would have to bring more and more meat for the priests and their families.

For anyone who knows history, that system of the priests benefiting from the sins of the people will sound very familiar; it became one of the infamous practices of the Roman Catholic Church in the selling of indulgences.

Back to Israel, though, with the priests profiting from the wickedness of the people, there was little to no incentive for them to try to get the people to actually live right.

And it showed:

Hosea 4:9 *And there shall be, like people, like priest: and I will punish them for their ways, and reward them their doings.*

Verse nine was God referencing the judgment that He had promised to bring upon Israel. The assumption would normally be that in any judgment, the priests would be far more protected than the people since they were God's men. But God made it clear that was not going to be the case; both priest and people would be equally judged, punished for their ways, and rewarded for their wicked doings.

God does not play favorites based on priestly garments or clerical robes or suits and ties.

Hosea 4:10 *For they shall eat, and not have enough: they shall commit whoredom, and shall not increase: because they have left off to take heed to the LORD.*

There are two different *theys* being spoken of in verse ten, both of which refer to the groups of people mentioned in verse nine. The first they, *they shall eat and not have enough*, refers back to the priests in verse nine. They were enjoying the sin of the people because that meant people would bring sin offerings for them to eat. God was going to judge them so that even when they did, they would not have enough, it would never satisfy. He would starve them with their cupboards full.

The second they, *they shall commit whoredom and shall not increase*, refers back to the people in verse nine.

Do you remember back in verse seven when God spoke of the people being increased? This verse is the answer to that verse. The people of Israel were haughty against God and not willing to obey Him, at least in part because they had increased numerically as a people and were therefore very strong and did not think they could ever fall. But here, in verse ten, God said that the people would commit whoredom and yet would not increase. In other words, you would think that when men across the nation were sleeping around with women everywhere, the population would increase. And yet, God was going to make sure that the exact opposite came true. He said that in spite of their promiscuity, they would not increase *because they have left off to take heed to the LORD.*

God tied their power through population growth to His blessings and favor on them. And as a sign and result of Him withdrawing that favor, they were going to experience a population implosion.

The oft-repeated phrase "demographics equal destiny" is only partially true in God's economy. A more accurate rendering of it would be "demographics influenced by Deity equal destiny."

Hosea 4:11 *Whoredom and wine and new wine take away the heart.*

Three negative things are mentioned by God in this verse. Whoredom means sexual sin, things like fornication, adultery, and prostitution.

Wine is mentioned next. It is from the word *yayin,* and here it indicates wine that is fermented, effervescent or bubbling, alcoholic.

New wine is next. It is from the word *tiyrowsh,* and it means juice fresh from the grapes. In fact, sometimes it is even still in those grapes:

Isaiah 65:8 *Thus saith the LORD, As the new wine is found in the cluster, and one saith, Destroy it not; for a blessing is in it: so will I do for my servants' sakes, that I may not destroy them all.*

There are a couple of things to take careful note of at this point. First of all, this is another indication that sometimes wine in the Bible spoke of that which was fermented, and sometimes it spoke simply of grape juice. People who want to use Scripture to justify drinking alcoholic beverages constantly point out that people were drinking wine, but they never point out that a lot of that wine was nothing more than unfermented grape juice.

The second thing to notice, though, is that God spoke even of that in a bit of a negative sense, lumping it together here with fermented wine and with whoredom. You see, while no one ever gets drunk from grape juice and therefore it is in and of itself not sinful, the children of Israel during the days of Hosea were so prone to drunkenness that God expected them to regard even unfermented grape juice as something to be avoided. And if He was that adamant about His people never even potentially becoming drunks, then there is no possible way for anyone to make a rational biblical case for drinking actual alcoholic beverages today.

Here is what God said of those three things in the list. He said that *Whoredom and wine and new wine take away the heart.*

He was not talking about the organ that pumps blood through our chest. As is the case in so many usages of the word *heart* in Scripture, He was using heart the way we often use it, as a euphemism for the inner man: the mind and the will and the emotions.

God said that whoredom and wine and new wine "take away" the heart. That phrase *take away* is from the word *lawkahk,* and among other things, it means to steal, to seize, to snatch, to capture. The same word is used in Judges 18:24 when Micah the idolater had his house robbed and chased after the Children of Dan, complaining that they had "taken" his gods. The same word is used in 1 Samuel 4:11, where the Ark of God was forcibly taken away from Israel in battle by the Philistines.

Sexual sins and booze will steal your heart, and not in a romantic sense. The implication is that they will make you a selfish, heartless monster. And that is exactly what happened to Israel. They became a nation of heartless people who were marked by theft and murder and whose clergy were okay with that because it kept their coffers and cupboards full.

No wonder God had a bone to pick with them.

Chapter Seven
Idolatry/Adultery, Adultery/Idolatry

Hosea 4:12 *My people ask counsel at their *stocks, and their *staff declareth unto them: for the spirit of <u>whoredoms</u> hath caused them to err, and they have gone a <u>whoring</u> from under their God.* **13** *They *sacrifice upon the tops of the mountains, and *burn incense upon the hills, under oaks and poplars and elms, because the shadow thereof is good: therefore your daughters shall commit <u>whoredom</u>, and your spouses shall commit <u>adultery</u>.* **14** *I will not punish your daughters when they commit <u>whoredom</u>, nor your spouses when they commit <u>adultery</u>: for themselves are separated with <u>whores</u>, and they *sacrifice with <u>harlots</u>: therefore the people that doth not understand shall fall.* **15** *Though thou, Israel, play the <u>harlot</u>, yet let not Judah offend; and come not ye unto Gilgal, neither go ye up to Bethaven, nor swear, The LORD liveth.* **16** *For Israel slideth back as a backsliding heifer: now the LORD will feed them as a lamb in a large place.* **17** *Ephraim is joined to *idols: let him alone.* **18** *Their drink is sour: they have committed <u>whoredom</u> continually: her rulers with shame do <u>love</u>, Give ye.* **19** *The wind hath bound her up in her wings, and they shall be ashamed because of their *sacrifices.*

    The story of Hosea and Gomer ended at the end of chapter three. For the first eleven verses of chapter four, God described the controversy that He had with Israel. The rest of chapter four will continue along the same lines but with a more narrow focus. That focus will be on the intertwined sins of idolatry and adultery that plagued the nation. In the text above, I have underlined eleven references to whoredom, and put asterisks beside seven references to idolatry. In just eight verses, eighteen references to idolatry and adultery!

God is about to make it very clear that idolatry breeds adultery which breeds more idolatry which breeds more adultery.

Dirty worship

Hosea 4:12 *My people ask counsel at their stocks, and their staff declareth unto them: for the spirit of whoredoms hath caused them to err, and they have gone a whoring from under their God.* **13a** *They sacrifice upon the tops of the mountains, and burn incense upon the hills, under oaks and poplars and elms, because the shadow thereof is good...*

It would be inaccurate to say that Israel had ceased to worship. They were still worshipping as much as ever; they had merely changed the objects of that worship. And as such, they had changed the objects of their inquiries as well. They used to ask the living God for His counsel on everything in their lives, but in the days of Hosea they were asking their stocks and their staffs for counsel.

Stocks were wooden gods that they had carved for themselves. And this was pretty handy from an economic sense because it was nowhere near as expensive as an idol cast or carved from silver or gold. So you could think of this as Dollar General idolatry, if you will; it was not of very high quality, but anyone could afford it.

Staffs were their walking sticks. When God said that Israel was having their staff declare unto them, He was talking about a practice called rhabdomancy, where people would use sticks in various ways to determine what the "gods" would have them do. Sometimes they would stand them all up and then let them go and see which way they fell. Sometimes they would take individual sticks and cut the bark off one side and then see if it landed bark side or bare side up, something like flipping a coin to determine heads or tails.

And those two things beg a rather significant question. Since Israel had the ability to have a relationship with and guidance from the true and living God, why in the world would they resort to figures that they cut out of stumps or sticks that they dropped on the ground?

God answered that question in the next words of verse twelve, *for the spirit of whoredoms hath caused them to err, and they have gone a whoring from under their God.*

The first thing we should deal with in this verse is the question, "What exactly is the spirit of whoredoms?" You see, there is a growing segment of thought in certain churches of our day concerning sin, namely that every sin is caused by some demon, some spirit that is responsible for getting people to engage in that particular sin. If you commit adultery, you have a demon of adultery. If you lie, you have a demon of lying. If you pick your nose, you have a demon that is a real booger...

But here is what James said:

James 1:14 *But every man is tempted, when he is drawn away of his own lust, and enticed.*

It is true that in passages like 1 Kings 22, certain spirits did push men along towards a particular sin. But that is an incredibly rare thing that we see in Scripture, especially compared to the overwhelming amount of times that God places the responsibility for our sin on us, our desires, our thoughts, and our spirits, meaning our attitudes and disposition toward something. And that is what God was saying through Hosea here when He used the word spirit. These people had a spirit, an attitude, a disposition toward whoredom.

"[They had] a general disposition on the part of all towards idolatry." (Jamieson, 471)

"[They had] a heart ensnared with whoredoms" (Linder: John Wesley Notes)

"They have in them a spirit of whoredoms, a strong inclination to that sin; the bent and bias of their hearts are that way; it is their own iniquity." (Henry, 4:1143)

So the reason these people were forsaking the living God in favor of asking counsel of stocks and staffs was because their carved wooden gods and their walking sticks never told them that they weren't allowed to commit physical or spiritual whoredom. And all the way back in the book of Numbers, with the matter of Balaam and the sin at Peor, sexual whoredom and spiritual whoredom always went together with them. They wanted to sleep around physically, so they slept around spiritually with other gods who would not tell them that they could not sleep around with other people. And part of that physical and spiritual whoredom, joined together, begins to be alluded to in the opening words of verse thirteen. *They sacrifice upon the tops of the mountains, and burn incense upon the hills, under oaks and poplars and elms, because the shadow thereof is good...*

This dirty worship tended to take place on mountains and hills and under shady trees like oaks and poplars and elms. In the Temple courtyards and complex, everything other than the holy place and most holy place was open and in view—light ruled rather than shadows. But when the people became intent on joining spiritual and physical whoredom together, only shadows would do for them, and we will see details of that in the last half of verse thirteen.

Debauched behavior

Hosea 4:13b ...*therefore your daughters shall commit whoredom, and your spouses shall commit adultery.*

This is what was happening under all of those nice, shady groves of trees where idolatrous worship was taking place. Daughters were committing whoredom, and spouses were committing adultery.

Here is how Keil and Delitzsch described that first part of it:

> "Therefore [Because of the shade, which afforded the ability to not be seen by all] the daughters and daughters-in-law carried on prostitution there. The worship of the Canaanitish and Babylonian goddess of nature was associated with prostitution, and with the giving up of young girls and women." (Keil, 81)

So daughters and wives were worshipping dirty, sensual little gods and were giving their bodies to filthy and sinful sexual pursuits in that worship.

The most profound and symbolic gift God ever gave man and woman was the gift of sexual intimacy; it is no wonder the devil has always sought to twist and pervert and throw it around publicly like scraps being thrown to the dogs.

So, how would God respond to this? Perhaps not like you may think:

Hosea 4:14 *I will not punish your daughters when they commit whoredom, nor your spouses when they commit adultery: for themselves are separated with whores, and they sacrifice with harlots: therefore the people that doth not understand shall fall.*

In order to understand this verse properly, you need to know who the pronoun "your" applies to, because that is who God is addressing in this verse. It referred to the husbands and fathers who were supposed to be the spiritual leaders of their homes. God said that He was not going to punish the daughters or the spouses, meaning the wives, because the fathers and husbands were doing the same things and worse. The fathers and husbands were *separated with whores, and they sacrifice with harlots.*

When husbands and fathers do not do right, it is no surprise at all to find wives and daughters who will not do right.

So God said that He was not going to judge them for their deep debauchery. And while that may sound like mercy, it was actually the exact opposite. Look at the last words of verse fourteen again:

...therefore the people that doth not understand shall fall.

If there had still been any hope, God would have judged them for their sin so that they could repent and be restored. But they had gotten to a place where God did not judge them for their sin, and that is the scariest place for any person or family or church or nation to ever come to. As long as God is still sending judgment, there may well still be hope. But when God has given up even attempting to correct us through judgment, there is absolutely nothing left but destruction.

Distinct Identities

Hosea 4:15 *Though thou, Israel, play the harlot, yet let not Judah offend; and come not ye unto Gilgal, neither go ye up to Bethaven, nor swear, The LORD liveth.*

A few hundred years before what we read here, this verse would not have made much sense to anyone reading it. You see, Israel used to be one kingdom of twelve tribes. But since the early days of Rehoboam, she was split into two distinct kingdoms, the Northern Kingdom of Israel and the Southern Kingdom of Judah.

Remember that Hosea was a citizen of the Northern Kingdom, Israel. And at this point, Israel was much farther gone than Judah was. She was so far gone that God describes her here as a harlot, a prostitute. She was so far gone that in the previous verse, God had promised not to even judge her for her iniquity, meaning He had simply given up on them.

So here, God, through Hosea, addresses Judah, the kingdom for which there is still some measure of hope. He tells Judah that even if Israel offends, they, Judah, don't have to. After saying that, though, He then says something that we definitely need to dig into, *and come not ye unto Gilgal, neither go ye up to Bethaven.*

Gilgal was pretty famous in Jewish history. It is the place where the covenant of circumcision was renewed in Joshua 5 after all the years of the wilderness wanderings. It therefore pictured the rolling away of the sin of a nation. Based on that, it would seem like a perfect place for Judah to go if they really wanted to get right with God and not follow in the sinful footsteps of Israel.

But many years after that positive scene in Gilgal, it became a hotbed of idolatry under Jeroboam II. In Hosea 9:15, God will say, *All their wickedness is in Gilgal.*

Bethaven is a bit of a riddle to unravel, but it is worth it. There was a city to the east of Bethel called Bethaven mentioned as far back as Joshua seven. But that is not the city being spoken of here. The minor prophet Amos, a contemporary of Hosea, in Amos 4:4-5 mentioned Bethel and Gilgal together as the centers of worship under Jeroboam II. Hosea has already mentioned Gilgal, but like Amos, he has also mentioned Bethel, just under another name. You see, Bethel was no longer worthy of its name because of their idolatry. Bethel means the house of God. But because of their idolatry, they were now euphemistically being called by the name of that other city nearby, Bethaven, which means the house of iniquity. God had basically uprooted their sign and said, "You are not worthy of that; let me give you one that fits."

So Bethel and Gilgal, two of the most positive and godly places from their past, had now been so twisted and corrupted by the idolatry of the present that God did not want His people, Judah, even walking onto the property.

I have seen that exact same thing happen in churches all over America, and it is always a tragedy when it does.

Not only did God not want Judah going to Gilgal or Bethel, in the last phrase of verse fifteen, He told them that He did not want them to swear, *The LORD liveth*.

Once again, on the surface, that is incredibly perplexing. Why would the LORD not want them to say that?

The answer is the same as the main thing for a business: location, location, location. It is not that He did not want them saying "The LORD liveth" at all; it is that He did not want them saying those words at Bethel or Gilgal. He did not want to debase His holy name by having it mentioned in either of those spiritual sewers.

Hosea 4:16 *For Israel slideth back as a backsliding heifer: now the LORD will feed them as a lamb in a large place.*

The word *for* that begins this verse ties back to the command that ended verse fifteen, the command that "the LORD liveth" should not be spoken at Bethel (Bethaven) or Gilgal. God did not want those words spoken there for, because, Israel was sliding back as a backsliding heifer.

Every reference in Scripture to some form of the word backsliding is found in Proverbs, Jeremiah, and Hosea. And yet, it is a perfect word to describe the spiritual condition of anyone in any age, including ours, who has been walking with God and then slides back from that position into a position of carnality and wickedness.

A backsliding heifer was one who was unmanageable and would not submit. And once again, that perfectly describes many saved people who nonetheless are no longer living on the outside to match what has taken place on the inside.

Whether nationally or individually, though, there will always be a price for that. And here is the price that God expressed at the end of verse sixteen, *now the LORD will feed them as a lamb in a large place.*

As with so many things we are seeing in this chapter, this initially seems like a head-scratcher, doesn't it? This sounds so peaceful, so wonderful. It sounds like something David himself would write in his closest moments with God.

And yet, that is the exact opposite of what this means and what this is like. The large place that God had in mind was the kingdom of Assyria. God was going to remove them from the protective walls of their cities and send them into captivity as a prey to the wolves. Adam Clarke said, "[This is] a species of irony. Ye shall go to Assyria, and be scattered among the nations; ye may sport yourselves in the extensive empire, wither ye shall be carried captives." (Clarke, 633)

But He still was not quite done with all of that yet:

Hosea 4:17 *Ephraim is joined to idols: let him alone.*

Ephraim was the largest of the ten tribes of the Northern Kingdom. Because of that, the Northern Kingdom often got called Ephraim in place of Israel. And that is what is taking place in verse seventeen. God said that Ephraim, the Northern Kingdom, was *joined* to idols. Joined is from the word *khabar,* and it means to be united to, to be coupled with. The idea is that of a union that is so strong that it cannot be given up. Ephraim, Israel, was not just dabbling in idolatry; they were delighting in it while drowning in it.

And God's simple answer to that was, "Let him alone." In other words, don't bother him, don't confront him, don't try to correct him, just let him go.

Again, the worst thing God can ever do is simply give up on you—and God had given up on Israel, all the while warning Judah not to be next.

Degraded conditions

Hosea 4:18 *Their drink is sour: they have committed whoredom continually: her rulers with shame do love, Give ye.*

There is some odd sounding terminology in this verse for us to work our way through. It begins with the phrase, "Their drink is sour." Without getting too graphic, this referred to people who got drunk enough to vomit and then wallowed in it and stank to high heavens from the alcohol and vomit combination. They were not just casual sinners; whatever sin they were involved in, they pursued it to the nth degree.

The next phrase continues that thought, *they have committed whoredom continually*. They had no casual sins; they were dedicated to all of their wickedness.

The last words of the verse are perhaps the most unusual of all to our Western minds: *her rulers with shame do love, Give ye.*

I would wager to say none of you have ever used a sentence like that in your normal day by day conversations a single time in your life.

We can begin to unravel those words this way. In the context of wickedness, when a ruler says, "Give ye," he is asking for a bribe. And that is what is being described here. Israel's rulers loved shame; they loved that which should bring shame, in this case, specifically bribery. So in one verse, we find drunkenness and perversion and bribery, not merely among the average people but among the people who were supposed to be in charge and leading the people right.

And the predictable end of all that would not be pleasant:

Hosea 4:19 *The wind hath bound her up in her wings, and they shall be ashamed because of their sacrifices.*

Keil and Delitzsch give a description of the first half of this verse that is both accurate and poetic: "The tempest has already seized upon the people, or wrapt them up with its wings, and will carry them away." (Keil, 84)

As to the last half of the verse, *they shall be ashamed because of their sacrifices*, the meaning is easy to discern by now. They had served their false gods because their false gods allowed them to do whatever they wanted. But in the end, they were going to be absolutely humiliated because of that choice.

Israel could have chosen the path of faithfulness—faithfulness to their spouses, faithfulness to God. Instead, she chose the path of unfaithfulness. And she found out the hard way what so many people are still finding out the hard way today: everyone gets to choose their own path, but no one gets to choose their own destination – the path they are on does that for them.

Chapter Eight
When God Cannot Be Found

Hosea 5:1 *Hear ye this, O priests; and hearken, ye house of Israel; and give ye ear, O house of the king; for judgment is toward you, because ye have been a snare on Mizpah, and a net spread upon Tabor.* **2** *And the revolters are profound to make slaughter, though I have been a rebuker of them all.* **3** *I know Ephraim, and Israel is not hid from me: for now, O Ephraim, thou committest whoredom, and Israel is defiled.* **4** *They will not frame their doings to turn unto their God: for the spirit of whoredoms is in the midst of them, and they have not known the LORD.* **5** *And the pride of Israel doth testify to his face: therefore shall Israel and Ephraim fall in their iniquity; Judah also shall fall with them.* **6** *They shall go with their flocks and with their herds to seek the LORD; but they shall not find him; he hath withdrawn himself from them.* **7** *They have dealt treacherously against the LORD: for they have begotten strange children: now shall a month devour them with their portions.* **8** *Blow ye the cornet in Gibeah, and the trumpet in Ramah: cry aloud at Bethaven, after thee, O Benjamin.* **9** *Ephraim shall be desolate in the day of rebuke: among the tribes of Israel have I made known that which shall surely be.* **10** *The princes of Judah were like them that remove the bound: therefore I will pour out my wrath upon them like water.* **11** *Ephraim is oppressed and broken in judgment, because he willingly walked after the* *commandment.* ***12*** *Therefore will I be unto Ephraim as a moth, and to the house of Judah as rottenness.* ***13*** *When Ephraim saw his sickness, and Judah saw his wound, then went Ephraim to the Assyrian, and sent to king Jareb: yet could he not heal you, nor cure you of your wound.* ***14*** *For I will be unto Ephraim as a lion, and as a young lion to the house of Judah: I, even I, will tear and go away; I will take away, and none shall rescue him.* ***15*** *I will go and return to my place, till they acknowledge their offence, and seek my face: in their affliction they will seek me early.*

From verses twelve through nineteen of chapter four, God had Hosea really bear down on the conjoined sins of idolatry and adultery that plagued Israel. People were committing spiritual whoredom because their little false gods would not call them into account for their physical whoredom.

He mentioned that once again in the verses above; but he went on to mention a consequence to that pursuit of false gods that they likely never anticipated, namely the fact that because of it, one day the real God would not be able to be found.

Universal judgment

Hosea 5:1 *Hear ye this, O priests; and hearken, ye house of Israel; and give ye ear, O house of the king; for judgment is toward you, because ye have been a snare on Mizpah, and a net spread upon Tabor.*

In Israel, as God laid things out, there was to be little if any difference between the secular and sacred. As a holy, chosen people, even their secular was to be sacred. And yet, on a practical level, everyone fit into one of three classes: the religious class, the ruling class, or the regular class. And all three of them are mentioned here. Verse one begins an address to the priests, the house of Israel, and the house of the king. In other words, absolutely everyone in Israel is being spoken to at this point. God told the priests to hear, the house of Israel to hearken, and the house of the king to give ear.

So absolutely everyone was being told the same thing in different words: "Listen up."

The last half of the verse told everyone why it was a very good idea for them to listen up:

"...*for judgment is toward you, because ye have been a snare on Mizpah, and a net spread upon Tabor.*"

That first phrase means, "Judgment is coming your direction, and it is going to fall on you." This judgment had a "because," specifically *because ye have been a snare on Mizpah, and a net spread upon Tabor.*

Snares and nets were traps designed to capture unsuspecting birds and animals. God accused the priests and the family of the king and the people themselves of entrapping the innocent into idolatry on the mountains of Mizpah and Tabor. Mizpah was on the eastern side of the Jordan River in the mountains of Gilead. Tabor was on the western side of the land in the territory of Zebulun. So from one side of the land to the other, God was angry with priests and kings and commoners who were calling people up to the high places to worship idols and ensnaring their souls in so doing.

It is bad enough when people serve false gods for themselves; it is infinitely worse when they tempt others to do so.

Hosea 5:2 *And the revolters are profound to make slaughter, though I have been a rebuker of them all.*

The first half of verse two is very enigmatic in its wording. So, what does it mean when it says, *And the revolters are profound to make slaughter*?

The revolters are the people who were in idolatry, knew it was wrong, and were luring others to it anyway. And they were not just casual about it; they were "*profound to make a slaughter.*" Profound means that they went out of their way, they were excessive about making a slaughter. And the slaughter they went out of their way to make was the slaughter of anyone who would not participate in their idolatrous religion. When it came to idols or Jehovah, they gave you two choices: serve the idols if you want to serve the idols or serve the idols if you do not want to serve the idols. And if you went looking for that third option, Jehovah, they would do everything in their power to take your life. And all of this was in spite of the fact that, as the end of the verse says, *though I have been a rebuker of them all.* The I in that phrase was Hosea, who, under God's direction, rebuked the priests and the politicians and the people—all to no avail.

Unhidden sin

Hosea 5:3 *I know Ephraim, and Israel is not hid from me: for now, O Ephraim, thou committest whoredom, and Israel is defiled.*

God here addresses the entire nation of Israel, and also calls her out by the name of her largest and foremost tribe, Ephraim. And He began with the very frightening phrases, *I know Ephraim, and Israel is not hid from me.*

Many of them undoubtedly believed that He did not know and that they were hidden. After all, as we observed in Hosea 4, they were committing their acts of religious prostitution under the shady groves of trees that they believed would hide them from prying eyes.

It would have been very helpful, perhaps, if they had read their own literature from a few hundred years before, given to them by the wisest of their kings:

Proverbs 15:3 *The eyes of the LORD are in every place, beholding the evil and the good.*

God saw, and God knew. He said, *O Ephraim, thou committest whoredom, and Israel is defiled.* Ephraim, their most prominent tribe, committed spiritual and physical whoredom, and Israel as a nation followed them into that defilement. They had a great influence – and they used it for all the wrong things and in all the wrong ways.

Hosea 5:4 *They will not frame their doings to turn unto their God: for the spirit of whoredoms is in the midst of them, and they have not known the LORD.*

The word frame, as used in this verse, is much the same in meaning as when someone says that they are framing up a house. It means to set a structure, to build in a particular way. Israel would not set the structure of their doings up in such a way as to return to God. Their deeds were preventing them from returning to God.

Such a thing should not be in the least bit surprising for anyone in our day who goes to church and pays attention. If you have ever seen someone who once seemed to be living for God and then turned and went full speed ahead into sin and absolutely would not repent and do right, you understand what this verse is talking about.

In spite of the faulty, mystical-sounding theology of some that separate our deeds from our "spirituality," those two things always go hand in hand. People choose to reject a relationship with the Lord because they want their wicked deeds more than they want the holy life He would expect of them. So they consciously choose their doings over truly turning to God.

Look at the last half of the verse again:

...for the spirit of whoredoms is in the midst of them, and they have not known the LORD.

They consciously choose their doings over truly turning to God, for, because, *the spirit of whoredoms is in the midst of them, and they have not known the LORD.*

This is the second time in the book that Hosea has mentioned the spirit of whoredoms. And just as in Hosea 4:12, here in Hosea 5:4 it is not talking about a demon that was making them commit adultery and fornication; it is talking about a predisposition of the heart. They would not turn to God because the predisposition of their heart was to sleep around both physically and spiritually. And Hosea marked that as proof that *they have not known the LORD*. It is not that they know Him and are simply disobeying Him; it is not that they used to know Him but do not know Him anymore; it is that they have not known Him. A life marked by sexual whoredom and spiritual whoredom is a life giving evidence of its lostness.

Unequal yoke

Hosea 5:5 *And the pride of Israel doth testify to his face: therefore shall Israel and Ephraim fall in their iniquity; Judah also shall fall with them.*

The phrase that starts verse five bears a bit of fleshing out. How is the pride of Israel testifying to his face, and whose face is being spoken of?

Let's take a look at another verse of Scripture that will shed light on this one:

Isaiah 3:9 *The shew of their countenance doth witness against them; and they declare their sin as Sodom, they hide it not. Woe unto their soul! for they have rewarded evil unto themselves.*

Isaiah 3:9 is saying the exact same thing as Hosea 5:5. In both cases, there was an openness of sin, no embarrassment or shame about it whatsoever, and the show of their countenance, the pride on their face, witnessed against them. The word witness in Isaiah 3:9 and the word testify in Hosea 5:5 are both from the word *awnah,* and that word means to speak, to shout, to testify, to respond as a witness.

So Hosea was using a bit of personification, picturing the pride of sinful Israel as being a witness that would get in their own faces and shout testimony against them. They could have chosen to humble themselves before the LORD, but instead, they chose to harden themselves in pride against Him. And here would be the result:

...therefore shall Israel and Ephraim fall in their iniquity;

As I have already explained, this was not only the last thing that anyone wanted to hear; it was also the last thing that anyone would quickly be willing to believe in the days of Hosea. All seemed well and prosperous within the kingdom. And yet, everything God said here came to pass.

But the real tragedy is found in the last phrase in verse five:

...Judah also shall fall with them.

There is something you should know about these words, and learning it will help you to understand a bit about the way Bible books were often written. Look back at Hosea 4:15:

Hosea 4:15 *Though thou, Israel, play the harlot, yet let not Judah offend; and come not ye unto Gilgal, neither go ye up to Bethaven, nor swear, The LORD liveth.*

We often get the idea that the writers of these prophetical books sat down one day and put pen to parchment, and finished up maybe late that night. But that was rarely if ever the case. In fact, in books like Daniel, we can see that the writing itself spanned many decades.

In Hosea 4:15, Judah was not quite so far gone; there was still hope for her. But by the writing of Hosea 5:5, God was saying *Israel is going to fall, and Judah is going to fall <u>with them</u>*. And it is in those two small words "with them" that we find a tragic unequal yoking. There was a time when Israel and Judah had been together and were supposed to be together. But now that they were split, and now that Israel was hell-bent on idolatry and adultery, Judah had no business being yoked with her whatsoever.

And yet, time and time again, she was. And though she did not fully fall until some years after Israel fell, it was the exact same sins that she learned from Israel that eventually caused her to fall.

Hosea 5:6 *They shall go with their flocks and with their herds to seek the LORD; but they shall not find him; he hath withdrawn himself from them.*

We now come to the verse that gives us our title for this chapter, "When God Cannot Be Found." What Hosea is describing in this verse is a time when his idolatrous, adulterous, backslidden people would realize that judgment and doom were coming and would suddenly "get a little religion" to try and fix things. They would run to their flocks and their herds and grab an animal to sacrifice to the LORD. But no matter how many animals they sacrificed, no matter how much incense they offered, no matter how much they reminded God that they were descended from Abraham Isaac and Jacob, they would not be able to find God because God would have withdrawn Himself from them.

And this is an accurate picture not only of what happened to them but of what can happen to any nation, any sinner, and even any backslidden Christian. There are deadlines that a nation can cross over that will assure their doom, there are deadlines that a sinner can cross over that will result in God never offering them the chance of salvation again, and there are deadlines that a backslidden Christian can cross over that will result in God going so far as to take their lives.

God told Noah that His Spirit would not always strive with man (Genesis 6:3). He told Israel through Isaiah that they must seek Him while He could be found and call upon Him while He was near (Isaiah 55:6). Any nation that believes that there will always be the opportunity to get right is foolish and will fall, any sinner that believes that there will always be the opportunity to get saved is foolish and will die and go to Hell, and any backslidden believer that believes there will always be a chance to get right understands nothing of Scripture or of God's character and will eventually be ruined.

Hosea 5:7 *They have dealt treacherously against the LORD: for they have begotten strange children: now shall a month devour them with their portions.*

This verse takes us back to the picture that God was painting for Israel through the relationship with Hosea and Gomer. Gomer, through her whoredom, had produced illegitimate children, strange children is the wording used here. Israel had done likewise. They had dealt treacherously against the LORD through their spiritual and physical whoredoms, and the result was that they, too, had produced strange children, children who grew up with the devil as their father rather than Jehovah God as their Father.

All of that is easy enough to understand. But the last half of the verse is another phrase that is a bit more obscure and bears a bit of delving into. God said that because of what they had done, dealing treacherously against Him and producing strange children, that *now shall a month devour them with their portions.*

A bit of an explanation as to how their system of borrowing and lending worked will help you to understand what was being said here. While our loans and interest in the Western world are normally figured in terms of a year, theirs were figured in terms of a month. (Jamieson, 475) In so many words, God was saying, *Time's up, the bill is now due, and everything you have is about to be devoured.*

Hosea 5:8 *Blow ye the cornet in Gibeah, and the trumpet in Ramah: cry aloud at Bethaven, after thee, O Benjamin.*

Three related places, three related activities, and one people group are mentioned or alluded to in this verse. The places are Gibeah and Ramah and Bethaven. And while Bethaven has been used before in the book of Hosea as a negative euphemism for Bethel, this one is actually Bethaven itself, and we know that because it was in the territory of the tribe of Benjamin, the people group that is mentioned in this verse.

All three of these places were in Judah. In three places of Judah, there was to be a cry of alarm sent up by the cornet, which was a curved horn of an animal used by shepherd; by the trumpet, which was a silver or brass instrument used by the priests and Levites during solemn occasions or to herald a cry of war; and by voices crying aloud.

And the warning that was to be shouted was the phrase *after thee, O Benjamin*. In our modern vernacular, that is the same thing as "They're after you, Benjamin!"

Just like Ephraim is used extensively throughout the book of Hosea as a name for all of the Northern Kingdom of Israel, Benjamin is used here as a name for the Southern Kingdom of Judah, mostly because her territory would be the first one to face the advancing Assyrian Army coming from the north. (Jameison, 476)

Hosea 5:9 *Ephraim shall be desolate in the day of rebuke: among the tribes of Israel have I made known that which shall surely be.*

Verse nine now bounces back to Israel again. God through Hosea told Ephraim (Israel) that they were going to be desolate in the day of rebuke, meaning the day that the Assyrians came against them. And when God said, *among the tribes of Israel have I made known that which shall surely be,* it meant that it was a done deal, and no amount of repentance or prayer could stop it at that point.

Jamieson, Fausset, and Brown put it this way: "It is no longer a conditional decree, leaving a hope of pardon on repentance; it is absolute, for Ephraim is hopelessly impenitent." (Jamieson, 476)

And now the scene will bounce back to Judah again:

Hosea 5:10 *The princes of Judah were like them that remove the bound: therefore I will pour out my wrath upon them like water.*

The princes of Judah is a way to refer to their rulers. And when it says that they were like them that remove the bound, it means the boundaries. Adam Clarke put it this way:

> "[They were] as execrable as they who remove the land-mark. They have leaped over law's enclosure, and scaled all the walls of right; they have despised and broken all laws, human and Divine." (Clarke, 634)

I would put it this way. They had torn down all of the fences others had erected before them without even bothering to ask why those fences had been put up to begin with. It would always be a good idea before we go tearing down fences to find out why they were there. And it is an even better idea, when we find out that a particular fence was put up by God Himself, that we simply leave it in place even if we have no idea why He put it there. He does know best, after all.

But because the princes of Judah tore down all fences and boundaries of morality, here is what God said He was going to do:

...therefore I will pour out my wrath upon them like water.

If you remember, God previously poured out His wrath on the whole world in Noah's day using water and on the entire Egyptian army at the Red Sea using water. So the picture He is painting here is of the fact that His wrath is going to be like a flood that absolutely wipes people out of existence.

The ruling line of Judah was ultimately decimated; they have not had a king on the throne for nearly three millennia now. And they will not until King Jesus sits on the throne of the Millennial Kingdom in Jerusalem.

And now things bounce back to the Northern Kingdom of Israel yet again:

Hosea 5:11 *Ephraim is oppressed and broken in judgment, because he willingly walked after the commandment.*

Oppressed and broken in judgment is not too hard to figure out. Ephraim, Israel, was going to be devastated by Assyria, and it was so certain of happening that it is stated here as a present tense reality even though it had not yet happened.

The last half of the verse will be confusing unless we understand whose commandment is being spoken of. Ephraim was oppressed and broken in judgment because he willingly walked after the commandment. That is clearly not the commandment of God being spoken of, otherwise he would have been blessed and unbroken rather than oppressed and broken.

This was the command of Jeroboam that the nation worship idols instead of Jehovah in 1 Kings 12:28-30. Israel, Ephraim, willingly followed that commandment. He did not have to have his arm twisted; he was an enthusiastic participant from the get-go.

But pay attention to the fact that all those many long years ago, God was already establishing the principle that if government ever decrees that we must go contrary to the law of God, we are bound by honor and righteousness to obey God and disobey government no matter what consequences government may lay upon us.

Sometimes a little rebellion is actually a good thing, not a bad thing.

Here is another set of divine consequences to what both Israel and Judah were doing:

Hosea 5:12 *Therefore will I be unto Ephraim* [Israel, the Northern Kingdom] *as a moth, and to the house of Judah* [the Southern Kingdom] *as rottenness.*

Both destructions by moth and their larvae and the rotting process are generally unseen destructions until it is too late. So even before the armies of the enemy came storming in, God was already going to be at work unseen in the darkness, weakening those kingdoms for that destruction.

Hosea 5:13 *When Ephraim saw his sickness, and Judah saw his wound, then went Ephraim to the Assyrian, and sent to king Jareb: yet could he not heal you, nor cure you of your wound.*

In different places throughout their history, as we read in Scripture, both the Northern and the Southern Kingdoms found themselves facing destruction by enemies, and rather than turning back to the LORD for help, they turned instead to other nations asking for help, nations that did not know God. That is what is being spoken of here in verse thirteen.

Jareb is only found twice in Scripture, both times here in the book of Hosea. And it is a nickname, not a historical name. Jareb means "an adversary." In 2 Kings 15, 2 Kings 16, and 2 Chronicles 28, we find Israel hiring Assyria to protect them from others. And yet it would be Assyria that eventually came and destroyed them. And that should have seemed predictable to Israel had they really thought it through. After all, if you do not have the physical ability to defend yourself against others, but you do have the ability to pay exorbitant sums of gold and silver to hire others to protect you by fighting against your enemies, why would those people not just save themselves the trouble and come and take your money without a fight instead since you clearly cannot do anything to stop them?

Oh, the ridiculous, illogical, foolish positions people find themselves in when they refuse to follow the Lord!

Hosea 5:14 *For I will be unto Ephraim as a lion, and as a young lion to the house of Judah: I, even I, will tear and go away; I will take away, and none shall rescue him.*

Israel doubtless thought that her real problem was with Assyria. But her real problem, her real adversary, at her choice, was God Himself. And God determined to be like a devouring lion both to the Northern Kingdom and the Southern Kingdom, and none would be able to rescue them from His destruction.

Unacknowledged offence

Hosea 5:15 *I will go and return to my place, till they acknowledge their offence, and seek my face: in their affliction they will seek me early.*

The final verse of this section is utterly straightforward. God was going to withdraw His presence from His people until they finally got willing to acknowledge their offense, their sin, and until they decided to truly seek His face again. And it would be their affliction that finally resulted in them doing so, and doing so early, not late in the day at the end of their list.

As long as their offense remained unacknowledged, there would be no healing, there would be no mercy, there would be no restoration.

Nor would God even be able to be found.

Chapter Nine
Coming Back To God—But Will It Matter?

Hosea 6:1 *Come, and let us return unto the LORD: for he hath torn, and he will heal us; he hath smitten, and he will bind us up.* **2** *After two days will he revive us: in the third day he will raise us up, and we shall live in his sight.* **3** *Then shall we know, if we follow on to know the LORD: his going forth is prepared as the morning; and he shall come unto us as the rain, as the latter and former rain unto the earth.* **4** *O Ephraim, what shall I do unto thee? O Judah, what shall I do unto thee? for your goodness is as a morning cloud, and as the early dew it goeth away.* **5** *Therefore have I hewed them by the prophets; I have slain them by the words of my mouth: and thy judgments are as the light that goeth forth.* **6** *For I desired mercy, and not sacrifice; and the knowledge of God more than burnt offerings.* **7** *But they like men have transgressed the covenant: there have they dealt treacherously against me.* **8** *Gilead is a city of them that work iniquity, and is polluted with blood.* **9** *And as troops of robbers wait for a man, so the company of priests murder in the way by consent: for they commit lewdness.* **10** *I have seen an horrible thing in the house of Israel: there is the whoredom of Ephraim, Israel is defiled.* **11** *Also, O Judah, he hath set an harvest for thee, when I returned the captivity of my people.*

There have been many words and phrases in the book of Hosea that we could honestly wish were not there. It seemed as if God's people could never quite bring themselves to acknowledge the problem from the heart. But as chapter six begins, we must acknowledge that the words themselves at the very least are exactly what they should have been.

A call to return

Hosea 6:1 *Come, and let us return unto the LORD: for he hath torn, and he will heal us; he hath smitten, and he will bind us up.*

The words of this first verse of the sixth chapter of Hosea do not come from nowhere; they are born out of the words of Hosea 5:14:

Hosea 5:14 *For I will be unto Ephraim as a lion, and as a young lion to the house of Judah: I, even I, will tear and go away; I will take away, and none shall rescue him.*

God said that He would tear His people and go away. So as chapter six dawns, the people acknowledge that tearing of God but then turn to the trust that the God who has torn them will heal them, and the God who has smitten and wounded them will bind those wounds. Based on that hope, the call goes out: *Come, and let us return unto the LORD*. Whether these were the words of Hosea only or of some of the people themselves is not clearly known; one way or the other, they were the right words.

Hosea 6:2 *After two days will he revive us: in the third day he will raise us up, and we shall live in his sight.*

As you might suspect, there is a dual reference within these words. On their face in the days of Hosea, they were an assurance that though the people had been devastated to the point of seeming dead, the LORD was so great that after a mere couple of days, He could revive them, and by three days time He could raise them back up completely, at which point they would determine to finally live in His sight rather than in the shadows of their sin.

These words, though, are also the only place in the Old Testament at which the third-day resurrection of Christ is hinted. It seems to be this very verse that is alluded to in 1 Corinthians 15:4:

1 Corinthians 15:4 *And that he was buried, and that he rose again the third day according to the scriptures:*

No other passage in the Old Testament fits the description of 1 Corinthians 15:4.

Hosea 6:3 *Then shall we know, if we follow on to know the LORD: his going forth is prepared as the morning; and he shall come unto us as the rain, as the latter and former rain unto the earth.*

Would God return and bless His people if they truly turned to Him with all their hearts? The clear belief that He would is shown in the words of this verse. But it could not be merely a temporary return for the purpose of securing those blessings; Hosea rightly pointed out in these words that there would have to be a following on of following the LORD. If they would do that, if they would determine to follow and then start following and then continue following, God would return to them just like the rains would return in their appointed seasons to heal the parched and dry ground.

A contradictory reply

Hosea 6:4 *O Ephraim, what shall I do unto thee? O Judah, what shall I do unto thee? for your goodness is as a morning cloud, and as the early dew it goeth away.*

God is now doing the speaking in verse four. And we find in His words an indication that, despite the proper call of verses one through three, many, if not most, of the people were not inclined to answer that call in the right way.

Speaking of their pious resolution in the first three verses, God proclaimed that goodness from them to be nothing more than the clouds and dew of the morning that seem so substantive and yet fade away in the light and heat of the rising sun. And that was going to bring a negative *therefore* rather than the positive *therefore* for which they hoped.

Hosea 6:5 *Therefore have I hewed them by the prophets; I have slain them by the words of my mouth: and thy judgments are as the light that goeth forth.*

It would be good if the words of God and of His men could be positive and comforting words at all times. But that cannot be the case and could not be the case in Hosea's day due to the people's propensity to proclaim their allegiance to the LORD and then turn right around and pursue their sin and idolatry. That being the case, the therefore God gave was *Therefore have I hewed them by the prophets; I have slain them by the words of my mouth.*

Both God and His prophets spoke the most cutting, uncomfortable, offensive words to the people. They felt like they were ripped to shreds and killed by those words, and those words did often lead to death by the judgment they proclaimed. And that part is much in view in the last phrase of the verse, *and thy judgments are as the light that goeth forth.*

This light was not a comforting light; it was the light that exposed sin and shined the way for the judgment to fall. It was a light they wanted to hide from, not a light they wished to bask in.

Hosea 6:6 *For I desired mercy, and not sacrifice; and the knowledge of God more than burnt offerings.*

This is one of the most unique passages in the Old Testament in that it is one of the few passages that Jesus quoted more than once during his earthly ministry:

Matthew 9:13 *But go ye and learn what that meaneth, I will have mercy, and not sacrifice: for I am not come to call the righteous, but sinners to repentance.*

Matthew 12:7 *But if ye had known what this meaneth, I will have mercy, and not sacrifice, ye would not have condemned the guiltless.*

In both of those passages and both of those events, Jesus uttered a cutting accusation to the religious leaders who stood against Him at that moment. They did not know what those words of Hosea meant. He, the carpenter, was accusing the scholars of the law of being biblically ignorant—and in this case, they were!

God, through Isaiah, pointed out to His people who had given lip service to returning that He expected mercy rather than sacrifice. We have repeatedly observed them oppressing the poor and doing injustice to those who could not defend themselves, all the while faithfully engaging in the religious ceremonies for God that meant nothing in the light of the way they were treating others who were made in God's image. Further, God said through Hosea that He desired *the knowledge of God more than burnt offerings.*

They offered, yes. They knew exactly what to offer and where to offer it and how to offer it. They just did not know, they did not really know, the God they were offering it all to. If they had, their behavior would have been very different. People who live in sin and oppress the weak know nothing of the God that their religious rights and rituals purport to point to.

Hosea 6:7 *But they like men have transgressed the covenant: there have they dealt treacherously against me.*

Were they not men? Yes, but they were supposed to be so much more; they were supposed to be God's men, all of them. They were supposed to be His holy, covenant people. But there, at the very altar of verse six where they sacrificed, they dealt treacherously against God. They said the right words, they made the right promises, and they meant none of it.

Hosea 6:8 *Gilead is a city of them that work iniquity, and is polluted with blood.*

For the first time in the book of Hosea, we find God calling Gilead out by name. The context of these words gives us indication that the Gilead being spoken of is Ramoth Gilead, a city on the other side of the Jordan River that was set aside as a city of refuge in Deuteronomy 4:43. People were supposed to be able to flee there and be safe until a proper trial could be held and then remain there in safety afterward if innocent. But here we find it polluted with blood, meaning that the people were ignoring God's command and the charter purpose for the city and shedding blood at will. It was utter iniquity through known disobedience.

Hosea 6:9 *And as troops of robbers wait for a man, so the company of priests murder in the way by consent: for they commit lewdness.*

God is still pointing out the violation of the city of refuge. The priests themselves were responsible for overseeing the safety of people to and within the city. But here, we learn that they had been corrupted and become susceptible to bribery for the purpose of murder. They themselves would meet a fleeing and desperate person on the way there, murder them, and receive their pay. They had become hit men for hire instead of protectors of people, and God regarded it as lewdness, a term that in other places is linked with the most perverted of sins.

Hosea 6:10 *I have seen an horrible thing in the house of Israel: there is the whoredom of Ephraim, Israel is defiled.*

Two hundred years previous, Jeroboam, the Ephraimite, had brought idolatry into the land. And here it was, still present and more prevalent than ever in the days of Hosea. God regarded it as a horrible thing; He regarded it as spiritual whoredom and said that Israel was defiled. No wonder her behavior was so corrupt, as we have seen in the last couple of verses.

Hosea 6:11 *Also, O Judah, he hath set an harvest for thee, when I returned the captivity of my people.*

Was Israel wicked and heading for judgment? Yes. But Judah was not to take these words against Israel as a sign that God was fine with her; her judgment, her harvest was coming as well, just a bit later than Israel's. The second invasion of Israel by Shalmaneser of Assyria, referred to here as God returning, or making return for the second captivity of His people, would serve as a herald to Judah that her harvest was just around the corner.

The question was, would turning back to the LORD matter? And in this case, sadly, the answer was no, simply because they turned back only in form and fashion and not in complete belief and changed behavior.

Chapter Ten
Of Kings and Bakers

In this text, take notice of two seemingly very different kinds of people and things: kings and ruling, bakers and baking.

Hosea 7:1 *When I would have healed Israel, then the iniquity of Ephraim was discovered, and the wickedness of Samaria: for they commit falsehood; and the thief cometh in, and the troop of robbers spoileth without.* **2** *And they consider not in their hearts that I remember all their wickedness: now their own doings have beset them about; they are before my face.* **3** *They make the *king glad with their wickedness, and the *princes with their lies.* **4** *They are all adulterers, as <u>an oven heated by the baker</u>, who ceaseth from raising after he hath kneaded the dough, until it be leavened.* **5** *In the day of our *king the *princes have made him sick with bottles of wine; he stretched out his hand with scorners.* **6** *For they have made ready their heart like an <u>oven</u>, whiles they lie in wait: their <u>baker</u> sleepeth all the night; in the morning it burneth as a flaming fire.* **7** *They are all hot as an <u>oven</u>, and have devoured their judges; all their *kings are fallen: there is none among them that calleth unto me.* **8** *Ephraim, he hath mixed himself among the people; Ephraim is a <u>cake not turned</u>.* **9** *Strangers have devoured his strength, and he knoweth it not: yea, gray hairs are here and there upon him, yet he knoweth not.* **10** *And the pride of Israel testifieth to his face: and they do not return to the LORD their*

God, nor seek him for all this. **11** *Ephraim also is like a silly dove without heart: they call to Egypt, they go to Assyria.* **12** *When they shall go, I will spread my net upon them; I will bring them down as the fowls of the heaven; I will chastise them, as their congregation hath heard.* **13** *Woe unto them! for they have fled from me: destruction unto them! because they have transgressed against me: though I have redeemed them, yet they have spoken lies against me.* **14** *And they have not cried unto me with their heart, when they howled upon their beds: they assemble themselves for corn and wine, and they rebel against me.* **15** *Though I have bound and strengthened their arms, yet do they imagine mischief against me.* **16** *They return, but not to the most High: they are like a deceitful bow: their *princes shall fall by the sword for the rage of their tongue: this shall be their derision in the land of Egypt.*

In Hosea 6, God painted a picture for the people of a time when they would seek after Him, but it would not matter because He could no longer be found. He is going to be continuing the picture of judgment in this passage, but this time through the seemingly odd conjoined pictures of kings and bakers.

A spurned hope

Hosea 7:1 *When I would have healed Israel, then the iniquity of Ephraim was discovered, and the wickedness of Samaria: for they commit falsehood; and the thief cometh in, and the troop of robbers spoileth without.*

There are many compound names of Jehovah found in the Old Testament. One of those very precious names is a name that God revealed to the children of Israel early in their relationship with Him:

Exodus 15:26 *And said, If thou wilt diligently hearken to the voice of the LORD thy God, and wilt do that which is right in his sight, and wilt give ear to his commandments, and keep all* *his statutes, I will put none of these diseases upon thee, which I have brought upon the Egyptians: for I am <u>the LORD that healeth thee</u>.*

The LORD that healeth thee is the compound name Jehovah Rapha. And I mention that because the word for healed in verse one is that exact same word, *rapha*. God is picturing Israel in her diseased and dying sinfulness and pointing out that not only did He have the ability to heal her, He desperately wanted to heal her. But when He would have done so, *then the iniquity of Ephraim was discovered, and the wickedness of Samaria.*

There is something you should know about that. This verse is not God saying, "I would have healed them, but oh wow, look what I just happened to find out about them." God already knew it all and knows it all. The word for discovered is *galah*, and it means to reveal itself. It is the exact same word used in 1 Samuel 14:8 when Jonathan said, "Behold, we will pass over unto these men, and we will discover ourselves unto them."

Putting all of that together, what was happening in Hosea 7:1 is that God was attempting to bring healing to the people: He wanted them to be healed, but the very act of Him trying to bring that healing resulted in the people revealing their wickedness even more. Keil and Delitzsch said it like this, "As the dangerous nature of a wound is often first brought out by the attempt to heal it, so was the corruption of Israel only brought truly to light by the effort to stem it." (Keil, 103)

God was sending them prophets and prophecies and warnings and judgments, trying to heal them of their sin, and all of that only made them more open and unashamed of their sin. It is not that they could not be cured; it is that they did not want to be cured. They liked their "disease."

The last half of the verse gives us a specific "for instance" of how they responded to God's attempt to set them right, saying, *for they commit falsehood; and the thief cometh in, and the troop of robbers spoileth without.*

God was trying to bring them into a condition of honesty, so they lied even more. God was trying to get them to respect people's homes and property, so they, under the cover of darkness, snuck into houses and stole even more. God was trying to get them to behave and be civil in the streets, so they produced more and more gangs of robbers brutalizing people in broad daylight.

Hosea 7:2 *And they consider not in their hearts that I remember all their wickedness: now their own doings have beset them about; they are before my face.*

The people were behaving like the people were behaving because they never even bothered to consider that God not only knew about all their wickedness but remembered all their wickedness. And that is obviously the reason lost people and carnal people behave like they behave today. They never bother to consider that God not only knows about all their wickedness but remembers all of their wickedness.

The last half of the verse is very interesting, saying, *now their own doings have beset them about; they are before my face.* Adam Clark gets that first phrase beautifully correct, saying, "Their own evil doings are as a host of enemies encompassing them about." (Clarke, 637) People live in sin and live in sin and live in sin, oblivious to the fact that all of their deeds have consequences and that all of those evils and consequences together eventually end up surrounding and destroying them.

That last phrase, *they are before my face*, means that God was seeing all of the things they were convinced He was not seeing. He was seeing all of them and all of their sins constantly. They were like little children holding their hands in front of their eyes, convinced that was hiding them from an all-seeing parent.

A stark picture

Hosea 7:3 *They make the king glad with their wickedness, and the princes with their lies.*

We now come to our first mention of the kings and rulers in this text, and it is not an encouraging mention. The rulers over God's chosen people, far from being disturbed and angry at the wickedness of the people, were instead thrilled with it all. Wickedness and lies served to keep people away from Jehovah and ensnared in the state-sponsored worship of idols.

Hosea 7:4 *They are all adulterers, as an oven heated by the baker, who ceaseth from raising after he hath kneaded the dough, until it be leavened.*

God now begins to bring the picture of bakers and baking into this discussion of sin among the people and their rulers. He proclaims everyone to be adulterers and then uses the descriptive phrase *as an oven heated by the baker, who ceaseth from raising after he hath kneaded the dough, until it be leavened.*

Here is what He meant by that. The people were so hot and inflamed in their passion for their sin, they were like a baker's oven that had gotten so incredibly hot that the baker was able to not even try to raise the temperature anymore. In fact, he was able to let it sit until the kneaded dough had become leavened, we would call it fully fermented, and was ready for baking. If you have ever baked bread, you know that can take anywhere from two to twelve hours. Long story short, that oven was incredibly hot—and so were the people's wicked, adulterous desires.

Hosea 7:5 *In the day of our king the princes have made him sick with bottles of wine; he stretched out his hand with scorners.*

Focus now shifts from the baker to the king. And what we find in verse five is a day referred to as the day of our king, meaning either his birthday or his inauguration day. On that day, the king's princes were getting the king drunk until he puked. The last phrase has to do with that; the king stretching out his hand with scorners was referring to them stretching out their hands to offer a drink to the king's health—which the king participated in, ironically ruining his health. The entire picture was one of debauchery at the highest levels, when the king and his princes were supposed to set the example of righteousness to the people.

Hosea 7:6 *For they have made ready their heart like an oven, whiles they lie in wait: their baker sleepeth all the night; in the morning it burneth as a flaming fire.*

We now come right back to the picture of baker and oven again. The word *for* that begins the verse takes us back to the sins already mentioned, things like adultery and drunkenness. With that understanding, the verse tells us that they have made their heart ready like an oven – they have heated it up, and it is ready to bake something.

The next phrase, *whiles they lie in wait*, means while they lay sleeping at night. So, if they are lying there sleeping, who is the baker who is also sleeping all night? The answer is, the baker is their lust and the fulfillment of their lustful desires.

In the morning, when they awake, the oven is still heated and ready; their heart is as anxious for sin as it was when they went to bed. They wake up, their baker wakes up, the oven is ready, it is go time to bake some sin.

The picture of ovens and bakers will continue in the next verse.

Hosea 7:7 *They are all hot as an oven, and have devoured their judges; all their kings are fallen: there is none among them that calleth unto me.*

They, meaning both the people and the rulers this time, as the context will show, were all as hot as an oven and had devoured their judges. Anyone who dared tell them what they were doing was wrong was a target. And when we read the words *all their kings are fallen*, anyone in Hosea's day was able to put names with that statement. Zechariah was murdered by Shallum, Shallum was murdered by Menahem, Pekahiah was murdered by Pekah, and Pekah was murdered by Hoshea.

Anyone wishing for the throne in those days had a death wish. And far from seeing the problem and calling out to God to find how He would have things done, the final phrase of the verse says, *there is none among them that calleth unto me.* No matter how bad it got, they would not call on Jehovah because He would demand repentance for their adultery, idolatry, and drunkenness.

Hosea 7:8 *Ephraim, he hath mixed himself among the people; Ephraim is a cake not turned.*

Here is yet another allusion to bakers and baking. God says that Ephraim has mixed himself among the people, and He likens that to them being a cake not turned.

Here is what He meant by that word picture. Ephraim, Israel, was mixing with the heathen Gentiles, adopting their ways and worshipping their gods. And this made them like a cake that was burnt on one side and raw on the other. The Easterners bake their bread on the ground, covering it with embers (1Ki 19:6), and turning it every ten minutes, to bake it thoroughly without burning it. (Jamieson, 483) If they neglected to turn it, it was worthless on both sides and all the way through.

A strength depleted

Hosea 7:9 *Strangers have devoured his strength, and he knoweth it not: yea, gray hairs are here and there upon him, yet he knoweth not.*

A few normally good commentaries miss the proper understanding of the word strangers in this verse, saying that it refers to the Assyrians and others who were invading. But in context, the verse just before this one spoke of Ephraim mixing himself among the people. And that is still what is being referred to in this verse. The heathen Gentiles they have intermingled with in idolatrous worship have devoured their strength; they are utterly weak, whereas they used to be strong – and they are too dull to even realize it. Completing that awful picture, God says that there are gray hairs all over their head, and they don't know that either.

Adam Clarke rather eloquently said of this:

"The kingdom is grown old in iniquity; the time of their captivity is at hand, and they are apprehensive of no danger. They are in the state of a silly old man, who through age and infirmities is become nearly bald, and the few remaining hairs on his head are quite gray. But he does not consider his latter end; is making no provision for that eternity on the brink of which he is constantly standing; does not apply to the sovereign Physician to heal his spiritual diseases; but calls in the doctors to cure him of old age and death! This miserable state and preposterous conduct we witness every day." (Clarke, 637)

Hosea 7:10 *And the pride of Israel testifieth to his face: and they do not return to the LORD their God, nor seek him for all this.*

This is the second time in Hosea that God has described the pride of Israel as testifying to their face, the first one being Hosea 5:5. And it once again means that the arrogant, proud look on their faces was a witness, an evidence, of just how much in the wrong they were. And yet in spite of all of that and the damage it was causing, they still would not return to or seek after Jehovah their God.

Hosea 7:11 *Ephraim also is like a silly dove without heart: they call to Egypt, they go to Assyria.*

Here is how Adam Clarke described this reference to Ephraim as a silly dove without heart: "A bird that has little understanding; that is easily snared and taken; that is careless about its own young, and seems to live without any kind of thought." (Clarke, 638)

That is exactly how they were. And because of that, they constantly called out to Egypt and Assyria for help rather than God—which made exactly as much sense as a bird calling out to the fowler for help.

A storm gathering

Hosea 7:12 *When they shall go, I will spread my net upon them; I will bring them down as the fowls of the heaven; I will chastise them, as their congregation hath heard.*

This referred back to what God said in the last verse about them running to Egypt and Assyria for help. God said here that when they go like a silly dove to either of those places for that purpose, He would be like a divine fowler, throwing the net over them and bringing them down to the ground. He was going to chastise them. And their congregation had indeed heard of this; it was written as a promise all through the books of the law and history that God would do that very thing when they forsook Him.

Hosea 7:13 *Woe unto them! for they have fled from me: destruction unto them! because they have transgressed against me: though I have redeemed them, yet they have spoken lies against me.*

Israel was doing as so many people do even today: running away from God rather than toward Him. And God's proclamation concerning that was *"destruction unto them!"* And a further reason for that was, in God's words, *because they have transgressed against me: though I have redeemed them, yet they have spoken lies against me.*

Israel transgressed against God. All sin is *against God.* That much everyone needs to understand. Sin is not a matter of harm done to others or social norms violated; it is always a violation that is against God.

God reminded them here that He redeemed them; this was a reminder that He bought them and brought them out of Egypt. And yet, in spite of that, we learn here that they had spoken lies against Him. We are not told here what lies He was thinking of or referring to, so commentators have felt quite free through the years to insert their ideas on this matter. And while they may be right, the specific lie is not the point, else God would have told us. The point was and is, anything we say about God that is untrue is a horrible thing.

Sadly, it is a thing that many God-haters feel just as free to do today as Israel did back then.

Hosea 7:14 *And they have not cried unto me with their heart, when they howled upon their beds: they assemble themselves for corn and wine, and they rebel against me.*

Howling upon their beds is quite the mental picture. Understand, though, that this is not howling as if they were wolves baying at the moon; this was howling in anguish because of famine and dearth. They were howling; they were even crying out to Jehovah in all of that howling. But it was not with their heart; it was not repentant—it was not sincere. They went from that bed of howling to assemble and rebel against God while calling out for wine and corn, meaning that they were crying out to their idols.

So they called out to Jehovah when no one was watching, but then when they got around the crowd they went right back to joining that crowd in their wickedness.

Hosea 7:15 *Though I have bound and strengthened their arms, yet do they imagine mischief against me.*

In verse thirteen, God said that He had redeemed them, yet they had spoken lies against Him. Here, he says that He had bound their arms, meaning to bind them up medically when they were injured. He had also strengthened their arms, and yet they imagined mischief against Him. Mischief means bad or evil. They literally wanted God hurt or destroyed.

God had been good to them; they hated Him in return.

Hosea 7:16 *They return, but not to the most High: they are like a deceitful bow: their princes shall fall by the sword for the rage of their tongue: this shall be their derision in the land of Egypt.*

God wanted the people to return. And they did, but not to Him; they returned to their idols instead. And yet, the God they were not returning to was the most High: there was and is none above Him. So God described them as a deceitful bow. This is one of only two places this epithet is used in Scripture, the other one being Psalm 78:57. A deceitful bow is one that looked right but did not shoot right. And that made it pretty but useless. And the result of all of this would be that *their princes shall fall by the sword for the rage of their tongue: this shall be their derision in the land of Egypt.* Their hateful mouthiness against God would result in them falling by the sword to Assyria and becoming a joke down in Egypt.

To put it all mildly, they needed better kings and better bakers.

Chapter Eleven
Sowing the Wind and Reaping the Whirlwind

Hosea 8:1 *Set the trumpet to thy mouth. He shall come as an eagle against the house of the LORD, because they have transgressed my covenant, and trespassed against my law.* **2** *Israel shall cry unto me, My God, we know thee.* **3** *Israel hath cast off the thing that is good: the enemy shall pursue him.* **4** *They have set up kings, but not by me: they have made princes, and I knew it not: of their silver and their gold have they made them idols, that they may be cut off.* **5** *Thy calf, O Samaria, hath cast thee off; mine anger is kindled against them: how long will it be ere they attain to innocency?* **6** *For from Israel was it also: the workman made it; therefore it is not God: but the calf of Samaria shall be broken in pieces.* **7** *For they have sown the wind, and they shall reap the whirlwind: it hath no stalk: the bud shall yield no meal: if so be it yield, the strangers shall swallow it up.* **8** *Israel is swallowed up: now shall they be among the Gentiles as a vessel wherein is no pleasure.* **9** *For they are gone up to Assyria, a wild ass alone by himself: Ephraim hath hired lovers.* **10** *Yea, though they have hired among the nations, now will I gather them, and they shall sorrow a little for the burden of the king of princes.* **11** *Because Ephraim hath made many altars to sin, altars shall be unto him to sin.*

In chapter seven of Hosea, God repeatedly brought up both kings and bakers. He was using the picture of bakers and baking and the hot ovens that they utilized to paint a picture of how hot for sin His people were, especially their rulers.

He will use a different word picture in this chapter to get the point across—different, but just as dire.

A terrible trumpet

Hosea 8:1 *Set the trumpet to thy mouth. He shall come as an eagle against the house of the LORD, because they have transgressed my covenant, and trespassed against my law.*

Take the thought of a cheerful-sounding musical instrument out of your mind as you look at the opening words of verse one. When God told Israel to set a trumpet to her mouth, it was not music He had in mind, it was mayhem. As is so often the case with the trumpet in Scripture, this is a trumpet of alarm, a trumpet designed to rouse everyone out of their sleep because doom was quickly beating down their way.

And it only took one more phrase for God to begin to identify that mayhem. There was a he who would come as an eagle against the house of the LORD. This he, though, was more than just a man. We know this because Moses already wrote of it many long years before Hosea did here:

Deuteronomy 28:49 *The LORD shall bring a **nation** against thee from far, from the end of the earth, **as swift as the eagle flieth**; a **nation** whose tongue thou shalt not understand;* **50** *A **nation** of fierce countenance, which shall not regard the person of the old, nor shew favour to the young:* **51** *And **he** shall eat the fruit of thy cattle, and the fruit of thy land, until thou be destroyed: which also shall not leave thee either corn, wine, or oil, or the increase of thy kine, or flocks of thy sheep, until he have destroyed thee.*

The particular eagle that was coming in Hosea's prophecy was not a man but a nation, the nation of Assyria. This was a nation whose tongue they indeed did not understand, and nation which had the fierce countenance spoken of here, and nation which showed no mercy to anyone as Deuteronomy 28:50-51 describes.

There is another term that we need to define, though. Hosea warned that this eagle would come against the house of the LORD. But remember that he was speaking to Israel, the Northern Kingdom at this point, not Judah, the Southern Kingdom. So this is not the Temple in Jerusalem that we are talking about; it is something different.

In the very next chapter, we find an explanation of what house he is talking about:

Hosea 9:15 *All their wickedness is in Gilgal: for there I hated them: for the wickedness of their doings <u>I will drive them out of mine house</u>, I will love them no more: all their princes are revolters.*

God mentions a geographical location within the land and then says that He will drive them out of His house. And they were not in the house of God in Jerusalem in those days, at all. So in this particular case, the Promised Land itself is the house that He was talking about. And that is exactly what He did, driving them out into Assyria into captivity.

The reason for this is found at the end of verse one, *because they have transgressed my covenant, and trespassed against my law.*

They would not obey. God gave them the covenant, they transgressed against it. The word transgressed (from *awbar*) basically means to walk across every line that He laid. God gave them His law, and they trespassed against it. The word trespassed (from *pasha*) means to rebel against. None of this was ignorance; it was a willful, rebellious choice to disobey God. That, not any vindictiveness on God's part, was what set that awful eagle in flight.

Hosea 8:2 *Israel shall cry unto me, My God, we know thee.*

There is a very fascinating New Testament tie-in to what we read here in verse two. God said that when Assyria, the eagle, finally arrived, bringing that awful judgment, Israel would look upward and cry out to God, "My God, we know you!" In other words "You can't do this, this isn't right, we really are saved!"

Here is the New Testament passage where we find very much the same thing:

Matthew 7:22 *Many will say to me in that day, Lord, Lord, have we not prophesied in thy name? and in thy name have cast out devils? and in thy name done many wonderful works?*

The subject is a judgment in both cases. In Hosea's day, with Israel, it was the judgment of the Assyrian nation falling on them and taking them into captivity. In Jesus' day, He was speaking of the final judgment, the Great White Throne, and people being cast into the lake of fire. In both cases, we see people claiming to know God, protesting that the judgment they are about to fall into is unjust. And in both cases, the problem was the exact same:

Hosea 8:3 *Israel hath cast off the thing that is good: the enemy shall pursue him.* **4** *They have set up kings, but not by me: they have made princes, and I knew it not: of their silver and their gold have they made them idols, that they may be cut off.*

Matthew 7:23 *And then will I profess unto them, I never knew you: depart from me, ye that work iniquity.*

They were living in sin. Israel, in Hosea's day, was engaging in idolatry, all the while claiming that they knew God and therefore the judgment against them could not possibly be right. The sinners who stand before Christ at the Great White Throne judgment are workers of iniquity, all the while claiming that they know Christ and therefore the judgment against them cannot possibly be right.

But the judgment was right in Hosea's day and will be right at the Great White Throne judgment. If there has been no change of the heart that has produced a change of behavior, then no one has the right to claim that they know God.

Intellectual understanding of the facts about God is not enough. As Keil and Delitzsch put it, "This knowledge of God, regarded simply as a historical acquaintance with him, cannot possibly bring salvation." (Keil, 112)

In verse three again, God said that Israel was not just involved in idolatry, they had actively cast off, thrown away the thing that is good. They wanted nothing to do with God's righteousness, God's law, God's covenant. They wanted their idols and God's blessings at the same time, and that was simply never going to happen.

In verse four, He pointed out that, rather than seeking His decision on their kings and on their princes, they simply chose their own kings and princes according to their own desires. In their very biggest national decisions, they did not even pretend to seek out God's counsel.

There was absolutely no evidence that they truly knew the God that they claimed to know.

A treacherous calf

Hosea 8:5 *Thy calf, O Samaria, hath cast thee off; mine anger is kindled against them: how long will it be ere they attain to innocency?*

Sin and the consequences it brings will forever be the most ironic of things. In verse three, God said that Israel, insultingly referred to as Samaria in this verse, had cast off the thing that was good. They had chucked God in the dustbin of their history in favor of their idols. But here in verse five, you can almost hear the head-shaking laughter of God as He says to Israel, "Thy calf, O Samaria, hath cast thee off." They deep-sixed the real God, and their false god deep-sixed them.

Their golden calf, so treasured by them, did absolutely nothing to help them in their day of despair. Whatever demonic and devilish power was behind that golden calf did absolutely nothing to help them in their day of despair.

Before a person ever decides that God is not for them, they really should examine the alternatives.

Having pointed out that their idol had forsaken them, here is what God said at the end of verse five: *mine anger is kindled against them: how long will it be ere they attain to innocency?*

God was angry with Israel because they pursued impurity rather than pursuing innocency. The phrase *attain to* (from *yakole*) means to struggle at something until you prevail. This is what God wanted to see from Israel concerning innocency in His sight. He wanted them not to be satisfied until He was satisfied.

And they were not even trying.

Hosea 8:6 *For from Israel was it also: the workman made it; therefore it is not God: but the calf of Samaria shall be broken in pieces.*

That unusual-sounding phrase at the beginning of this verse, *for from Israel was it also*, means that it, that golden calf, was from Israel; Israel made it; Israel created it. And that leads to the next logical phrase: *the workman made it; therefore it is not of God.*

God does not make idols. He may make something that you turn into an idol, but if you have an idol, no matter what it is, God did not make it. And because of that, He said, *but the calf of Samaria shall be broken in pieces.*

Neither the golden calf of Bethel or the golden calf of Dan exists anymore. It never helped Israel in the least, no matter how much they called out to it, and it was at some point broken into pieces, just as God said.

A trouble multiplied

Hosea 8:7 *For they have sown the wind, and they shall reap the whirlwind: it hath no stalk: the bud shall yield no meal: if so be it yield, the strangers shall swallow it up.*

The *they* in this verse refers back to Israel once again. Through their idolatry and disobedience and rebellion, they have sown the wind, a seemingly pleasant thing. But what they will reap from that sowing is the whirlwind, the devastating tornado. Just like the farmer's seed produces a much larger plant and crop of fruit, the sinner's seed does the same.

That sin that you treasure will bring judgment out of measure.

The last half of the verse ties in with that picture. This destroying whirlwind will wreck the life-giving crops that they have been trying to grow. And even if anything does manage to grow, strangers, the invading Assyrians, will eat it.

Hosea 8:8 *Israel is swallowed up: now shall they be among the Gentiles as a vessel wherein is no pleasure.*

Notice the way God expresses the time in this verse. While Israel was still there in their land, God said that she is, right now, swallowed up. He said *now shall they be among the Gentiles*. He was expressing a future event as a present certainty because it was. They had passed the point of no return, and nothing would stay the judgment at this point.

They would be dispersed among the Gentiles. And when they got there into Gentile lands, they would find themselves regarded as a vessel wherein is no pleasure.

Do you understand how drastic of a fall that is? Look at what God said of them when He first made them a nation:

Exodus 19:5 *Now therefore, if ye will obey my voice indeed, and keep my covenant, then ye shall be <u>a peculiar treasure unto me above all people</u>: for all the earth is mine:*

They were a treasure to God; they became trash to their captors. The picture is of a rotten, rancid, putrid vessel that nobody wants to put anything in and no one would ever dare drink out of. This is what they became among the Gentiles.

Oh, the depths of degradation sin can take a person or a people to!

Hosea 8:9 *For they are gone up to Assyria, a wild ass alone by himself: Ephraim hath hired lovers.*

There was history behind what Hosea said here. Israel had indeed "gone up to Assyria," meaning to go to them for help:

2 Kings 15:19 *And Pul the king of Assyria came against the land: and Menahem gave Pul a thousand talents of silver, that his hand might be with him to confirm the kingdom in his hand.*

Menahem hired Assyria's help to establish himself on the throne of Israel; this thing of hiring Assyria or other pagan nations for help was a regular practice with them during the latter years of the kingdom. And here is how God described them and what they were doing in the last half of the verse:

...a wild ass alone by himself: Ephraim hath hired lovers.

The wild ass pictures an ungoverned, untamable beast. And this is what Ephraim (Israel) was like as she hired her lovers, meaning as she hired all of these foreign nations. You could have smacked her across the head with a 2 x 4, and she would not have changed.

Hosea 8:10 *Yea, though they have hired among the nations, now will I gather them, and they shall sorrow a little for the burden of the king of princes.*

Putting some names with the pronouns in verse ten will help you to understand the verse:

Hosea 8:10 *Yea, though they* [Israel] *have hired among the nations, now will I gather them* [The nations they have hired], *and they* [Israel] *shall sorrow a little for the burden of the king of princes.*

Here is what God was saying. Rather than returning to Him, Israel continually went to pagan, heathen nations and sought their favor by paying them off. But in spite of that, God was going to gather those nations that they had hired and bring them against Israel in judgment, and Israel was going to be sorrowful because of the financial burden the king of their princes constantly put them under.

And here is one of the places we find that happening in history. I gave you one of the verses earlier; here are both of them together that show the entire picture:

2 Kings 15:19 *And Pul the king of Assyria came against the land: and Menahem gave Pul a thousand talents of silver, that his hand might be with him to confirm the kingdom in his hand.* **20** *And <u>Menahem exacted the money of Israel</u>, even of all the mighty men of wealth, of each man fifty shekels of silver, to give to the king of Assyria. So the king of Assyria turned back, and stayed not there in the land.*

When it comes to things that are good and valuable, sin doesn't pay; it costs.

Hosea 8:11 *Because Ephraim hath made many altars to sin, altars shall be unto him to sin.*

Here is the history behind what we read in verse eleven, described by Adam Clarke.

> "Though it does not appear that the Jews in Babylon were obliged to worship the idols of the country, except in the case mentioned by Daniel, yet it was far otherwise with the Israelites in Assyria, and the other countries of their dispersion. Because they had made many altars to sin while they were in their own land, they were obliged to continue in the land of their captivity a similar system of idolatry against their will. Thus they felt and saw the evil of their

idolatry, without power to help themselves."
(Clarke, 640)

I would put it this way. What they would not give up, they eventually could not give up. God judged them, not by taking away their sin, but by placing them in a situation in which it would be crammed down their throats until they were sick to death of it.

They sowed the wind. They reaped the whirlwind.

Chapter Twelve
Wanderers Among the Nations

Hosea 9:1 *Rejoice not, O Israel, for joy, as other people: for thou hast gone a whoring from thy God, thou hast loved a reward upon every cornfloor.* **2** *The floor and the winepress shall not feed them, and the new wine shall fail in her.* **3** *They shall not dwell in the LORD'S land; but Ephraim shall return to Egypt, and they shall eat unclean things in Assyria.* **4** *They shall not offer wine offerings to the LORD, neither shall they be pleasing unto him: their sacrifices shall be unto them as the bread of mourners; all that eat thereof shall be polluted: for their bread for their soul shall not come into the house of the LORD.* **5** *What will ye do in the solemn day, and in the day of the feast of the LORD?* **6** *For, lo, they are gone because of destruction: Egypt shall gather them up, Memphis shall bury them: the pleasant places for their silver, nettles shall possess them: thorns shall be in their tabernacles.* **7** *The days of visitation are come, the days of recompence are come; Israel shall know it: the prophet is a fool, the spiritual man is mad, for the multitude of thine iniquity, and the great hatred.* **8** *The watchman of Ephraim was with my God: but the prophet is a snare of a fowler in all his ways, and hatred in the house of his God.* **9** *They have deeply corrupted themselves, as in the days of Gibeah: therefore he will remember their iniquity, he will visit their sins.* **10** *I found Israel like grapes in the wilderness; I saw* *your fathers as the firstripe in the fig tree at her first time: but they went to Baalpeor, and separated themselves unto that shame; and their abominations were according as they loved.* **11** *As for Ephraim, their glory shall fly away like a bird, from the birth, and from the womb, and from the conception.* **12** *Though they bring up their children, yet will I bereave them, that there shall not be a man left: yea, woe also to them when I depart from them!* **13** *Ephraim, as I saw Tyrus, is planted in a pleasant place: but Ephraim shall bring forth his children to the murderer.* **14** *Give them, O LORD: what wilt thou give? give them a miscarrying womb and dry breasts.* **15** *All their wickedness is in Gilgal: for there I hated them: for the wickedness of their doings I will drive them out of mine house, I will love them no more: all their princes are revolters.* **16** *Ephraim is smitten, their root is dried up, they shall bear no fruit: yea, though they bring forth, yet will I slay even the beloved fruit of their womb.* **17** *My God will cast them away, because they did not hearken unto him: and they shall be wanderers among the nations.*

In chapter eight, God told Israel that she had sown the wind, but would reap the whirlwind. And one of the devastating ways that was going to play out will be discussed here in chapter nine as God describes their coming captivity and dispersion.

A command to sorrow

Hosea 9:1 *Rejoice not, O Israel, for joy, as other people: for thou hast gone a whoring from thy God, thou hast loved a reward upon every cornfloor.*

In the very beginning days of the Jewish monarchy, Israel had expressed a wrong desire, one that she unfortunately never rid herself of:

1 Samuel 8:5 *And said unto him, Behold, thou art old, and thy sons walk not in thy ways: now make us a king to judge us **like all the nations**.*

This thing of wanting to be like the heathen, Gentile nations around them was a rot in the soul of Jewish life. And God through Hosea deals with it again here in verse five, telling them, *Rejoice not, O Israel, for joy, as other people.*

This was clearly a situational rather than a perpetual command. There are many other instances in the Old Testament in which God plainly instructed His people to rejoice. The issue here was them rejoicing "as other people." Israel was to rejoice in holiness and in the blessings of God that came from that life of holiness. Instead, she was now rejoicing over very different things:

Hosea 10:5 *The inhabitants of Samaria shall fear because of the calves of Bethaven: for the people thereof shall mourn over it, and the priests thereof that **rejoiced** on it, for the glory thereof, because it is departed from it.*

Israel's rejoicing was, in the days of Hosea, rejoicing "as other people." The heathens rejoiced in idols and so did Israel. The heathens rejoiced in wicked alliances and so did Israel. She had devolved to a level of degradation in which if it made God happy, it made them unhappy, and if it made the devil happy, it made them happy.

In short, she had become much like America today.

And it will not turn out any better for us than it did for them.

At the end of verse one, God once again tied sexual sins and idolatry together, just as He has done throughout the book, saying, *For thou hast gone a whoring from thy God, thou hast loved a reward upon every cornfloor.* The dual picture painted here is of prostitution and payment in public places and of their spiritual prostitution with their idols that they expected to result in great harvests. As the next verse will show, that was a foolish hope indeed:

Hosea 9:2 *The floor and the winepress shall not feed them, and the new wine shall fail in her.*

John Wesley observed, "Samaria and all Israel expect a full vintage, but they expect it from their idols, and therefore shall be disappointed." (Linder: John Wesley's Notes)

Both in corn and wine, Israel was going to find out that her idols *could not* produce for her, and Jehovah *would not* produce for her because of those idols. And thus, the God who so often instructed His people to shout and rejoice, now commands them to sorrow instead. They are to sorrow for their sin, and they are to sorrow for the devastation that sin has wrought.

A coming dispersion

Hosea 9:3 *They shall not dwell in the LORD'S land; but Ephraim shall return to Egypt, and they shall eat unclean things in Assyria.*

Israel, unlike any other nation in the history of the world, was given an unheard-of gift on a silver platter. She was given a land and the assurance that the one singular thing she would ever need to do to keep it was simply to obey God. She could have had an army made up of two blind old men with one crooked stick between them as a weapon, and all the nations of the earth could never defeat her if she would simply do that one thing.

And yet they had now reached the days when Hosea was having to tell them that they would no longer dwell in that land. Ephraim, put here again for Israel, was going to end up both back in Egypt, where she began, and also eating *unclean things in Assyria.*

This return to Egypt would be a punishment, not a refuge:

Hosea 8:13 *They sacrifice flesh for the sacrifices of mine offerings, and eat it; but the LORD accepteth them not; now will he remember their iniquity, and visit their sins: they shall return to Egypt.*

The eating of unclean things in Assyria showed them being reduced to what, for them, was a sign of savagery. To find themselves surviving on pork and other filthy animals was an unspeakable thing. And yet, that is exactly what sin consistently does, reducing people to levels of humiliation they once could never have fathomed.

Hosea 9:4 *They shall not offer wine offerings to the LORD, neither shall they be pleasing unto him: their sacrifices shall be unto them as the bread of mourners; all that eat thereof shall be polluted: for their bread for their soul shall not come into the house of the LORD.*

There are several levels of degradation shown in this verse, a picture of what life would be like for them in Assyria. We first of all find that they would not offer wine offerings to the LORD, and they would not be pleasing to Him. These two things go together; the first phrase is the effect, the second is the cause. Since Israel had forsaken Jehovah in favor of idols, they were not and would not be pleasing to Him. And since this resulted in their removal from their land, they would no longer have their vineyards and therefore there would be no more of the drink offerings proscribed in Leviticus 23:13 and many other places in the law. This powerful symbol of prosperity and joy was going to be merely a distant, wistful memory to them in their captivity and dispersion.

The next level of their degradation is found in the words *their sacrifices shall be unto them as the bread of mourners; all that eat thereof shall be polluted:*

The Family Bible notes points out from Deuteronomy 26:14 that "Persons mourning for the dead, with all that they ate, were regarded as unclean. No offering could be made from their food for any holy purpose." (Linder: Family Bible Notes)

In Assyria, all of them were going to be mourning for the dead, a mourning that would continue for longer than any of them could have imagined.

The third level of their degradation is found in the final words of verse four, *for their bread for their soul shall not come into the house of the LORD.* They were removed from their land, and the house of God that they had refused to go to was now forever unavailable to them. They *would not* come and offer their sacrifices, and now they *could not* come and offer their sacrifices.

That thought continues into the next two verses.

Hosea 9:5 *What will ye do in the solemn day, and in the day of the feast of the LORD? 6 For, lo, they are gone because of destruction: Egypt shall gather them up, Memphis shall bury them: the pleasant places for their silver, nettles shall possess them: thorns shall be in their tabernacles.*

Back in chapter two, God had spoken through Hosea to Gomer and beyond Gomer making this ominous promise:

Hosea 2:11 *I will also cause all her mirth to cease, her feast days, her new moons, and her sabbaths, and all her solemn feasts.*

Those words are now echoed more forcefully here in Hosea 9:5. God was going to separate Israel from her three greatest holy days of the year. Again, John Wesley said that this spoke of "Her solemn feasts—the three annual feasts of tabernacles, weeks, and Passover, all which ceased when they were carried captive, by Salmaneser." (Linder: John Wesley's Notes)

God asks here what they are going to do in those days. What are they going to do in Assyria when their heart finally longs for what they once had and was now gone forever? In verse six, God elaborates on that loss, saying, *For, lo, they* [the people who would now want to worship] *are gone because of destruction: Egypt shall gather them up, Memphis shall bury them.*

The destruction of the land led many to flee into Egypt. They were fleeing to they knew not what. Egypt would indeed "gather them up." But the very next phrase lets us know what that "gathering up" would entail, saying, *"Memphis shall bury them."*

In Bible times, Memphis was also called Noph. In our day, it is Cairo. And it was famed as a necropolis – a place for the dead. (Jamieson, 489) They would flee into Egypt hoping to live, not realizing they were running into a graveyard—their graveyard.

And here is what they would leave behind: *the pleasant places for their silver, nettles shall possess them: thorns shall be in their tabernacles.*

Their pleasant homes, places where they in their wealth stored their silver, would be left desolate and taken over by nettles, thistles. Their tabernacles, another word for tents or dwelling places, would be taken over by thorns.

Hosea 9:7 *The days of visitation are come, the days of recompence are come; Israel shall know it: the prophet is a fool, the spiritual man is mad, for the multitude of thine iniquity, and the great hatred.*

Visitation is mentioned fifteen times in Scripture, and the vast bulk of those fifteen times are negative, indicating that the God who is "visiting" them is bringing punishment with Him. That is clearly the case here since God follows up with the words *"the days of recompence are come."* Israel is about to receive the payment in full for her iniquity and idolatry.

"Israel shall know it," God says. This will not be a hidden thing; it will not be something that people have to spread the word about. It will be known by all.

At this point in the monologue, God segues into a discussion of those who should have been trying to head this off at the pass all along: the clergy. He says, *the prophet is a fool, the spiritual man is mad, for the multitude of thine iniquity, and the great hatred.*

The prophet, the man who should have spoken the words of God to the people, has instead spoken his own words. He is a fool, and all of his predictions of peace and victory are going to be openly mocked as they so clearly miss in every regard.

The spiritual man, the man who pretended to be operating under the influence of the Holy Spirit, is mad. And while mad in the Scripture often indicates insanity, it here indicates bitter anger. Adam Clarke said, "He is now enraged to see every thing falling out contrary to his prediction." (Clarke, 642)

The last part of the verse, *for the multitude of thine iniquity, and the great hatred,* shows the cause of these "spiritual men" failing so spectacularly. Because of the multitude of their iniquity, and because of how badly God hates it, they have been given over to hirelings, corrupt clergy, people who make a living by lying.

Be warned: America is largely in that same place now.

In June of 2023, the "Reverend" Emily Bowen-Marler of Brentwood Christian Church, rewrote some of the parables of Jesus, preaching, "The empire of God is like the queer youth who challenged the confines of binary thinking and tore down the rigid parameters of masculine and feminine, diffusing the toxicity that has plagued communities of faith for generations until the spectrum of gender diversity was lived into and celebrated as far as the eye could see...

"The empire of God is like the trans woman athlete whose presence on the women's team helped strengthen the bonds of trust and compassion, which buoyed all of their confidence as a team, with all players feeling empowered to be their best and made them an unstoppable force in their sport." (Woke Pastor, 2024)

Let all of that sink in. A lost woman in the service of Satan calls herself a pastor, rewrites the very words of Jesus to say the exact opposite things that Scripture repeatedly says, and has people listening to and believing her.

Andy Stanley, pastor of Northpoint church in Georgia, in a sermon that went viral just a few years ago, said, among other things:

> "It is next to impossible to defend the entire Bible."

> "Jesus loves me, this I know, for the Bible tells me so … This is where our trouble begins."

> "...such things as the fall of Jericho, Noah's flood, and the exodus of Israel from Egypt cannot be verified, have not been confirmed by archaeology, and are spurious examples of stories in the Bible that conflict with what everyone knows." (Ahlheim, 2016)

This is one of the most popular, respected ministers in America. I want to believe that he means well and is merely misguided. But whether that is the case or not, he is openly wrecking people's confidence in Scripture, and people are eating it up.

Leading the putrid prophet brigade is no less a personage than Pope Francis, the unabashedly heretical leader of the Catholic church as of now. Earlier this month (September 2024) he was speaking to young people at an interfaith gathering in Singapore. In that talk, he said, "There is only one God, and each of us has a language to arrive at God. Some are Sikh, Muslim, Hindu, Christian, and they are different paths to God." (Ayers, 2024)

If only Jesus had known this; it maybe would have kept Him from saying such non-pope-approved things as *"I am the way, the truth, and the life: no man cometh unto the Father, but by me."* In fact, it would have even kept Him from dying for us since there were already plenty of other ways for man to be saved!

Because of the multitude of Israel's iniquity, and because of how badly God hated it, they were given over to hirelings, corrupt clergy, people who made a living by lying.

Because of the multitude of our iniquity, and because of how badly God hates it, we have been given over to hirelings, corrupt clergy, people who make a living by lying.

Hosea 9:8 *The watchman of Ephraim was with my God: but the prophet is a snare of a fowler in all his ways, and hatred in the house of his God.*

There is a division in verse eight that should not be there. Not in the grammar; that, as in all of Scripture, is perfect. No, the division that should not be here is the division between watchman and prophet.

In better days, God was able to look to prophets like Ezekiel and say things like this:

Ezekiel 3:17 *Son of man, I have made thee a* **watchman** *unto the house of Israel: therefore hear the word at my mouth, and give them warning from me.*

But by the time of Hosea, the prophet as a watchman, warning the people of their sin and God's impending judgment on them for that sin, was quickly becoming a thing of the past. Hosea himself clearly fit that bill, but he was one of very few. It was a time when God was now saying, *"The watchman of Ephraim* **was** *with my God:* **but** *the prophet* **is** *a snare of a fowler in all his ways, and hatred in the house of his God.*

Rather than being a deliverer of the people through the telling of painful truths, the prophets had become devourers of the people through the telling of pleasant lies. They had become snares of fowlers—traps for silly birds—or, in this case, people who were behaving like silly birds. And he was doing this out of hatred in the house of his God; he despised God, God's house, God's commandments, and God's ways.

Hosea 9:9 *They have deeply corrupted themselves, as in the days of Gibeah: therefore he will remember their iniquity, he will visit their sins.*

Gibeah may not be very familiar to the average Christian; it is not exactly a famous and oft-mentioned place of Scripture. But everyone back then knew it very well. And when you look back in Scripture at what he was talking about, you will have some sense of how far Israel had fallen in the days of Hosea. Here is what God was comparing Israel to:

Judges 19:16 *And, behold, there came an old man from his work out of the field at even, which was also of mount Ephraim; and he sojourned in Gibeah: but the men of the place were Benjamites.* **17** *And when he had lifted up his eyes, he saw a wayfaring man in the street of the city: and the old man said, Whither goest thou? and whence comest thou?* **18** *And he said unto him, We are passing from Bethlehemjudah toward the side of mount Ephraim; from thence am I: and I went to Bethlehemjudah, but I am now going to the house of the LORD; and there is no man that receiveth me to house.* **19** *Yet there is both straw and provender for our asses; and there is bread and wine also for me, and for thy handmaid, and for the young man which is with thy servants: there is no want of any thing.* **20** *And the old man said, Peace be with thee; howsoever let all thy wants lie upon me; only lodge not in the street.* **21** *So he brought him into his house, and gave provender unto the asses: and they washed their feet, and did eat and drink.* **22** *Now as they were making their hearts merry, behold, the men of the city, certain sons of Belial, beset the house round about, and beat at the door, and spake to the master of the house, the old man, saying, Bring forth the man that came into thine house, that we may know him.* **23** *And the man, the master of the house, went out unto them, and said unto them, Nay, my brethren, nay, I pray you, do not so* *wickedly; seeing that this man is come into mine house, do not this folly.* **24** *Behold, here is my daughter a maiden, and his concubine; them I will bring out now, and humble ye them, and do with them what seemeth good unto you: but unto this man do not so vile a thing.* **25** *But the men would not hearken to him: so the man took his concubine, and brought her forth unto them; and they knew her, and abused her all the night until the morning: and when the day began to spring, they let her go.* **26** *Then came the woman in the dawning of the day, and fell down at the door of the man's house where her lord was, till it was light.* **27** *And her lord rose up in the morning, and opened the doors of the house, and went out to go his way: and, behold, the woman his concubine was fallen down at the door of the house, and her hands were upon the threshold.* **28** *And he said unto her, Up, and let us be going. But none answered. Then the man took her up upon an ass, and the man rose up, and gat him unto his place.* **29** *And when he was come into his house, he took a knife, and laid hold on his concubine, and divided her, together with her bones, into twelve pieces, and sent her into all the coasts of Israel.* **30** *And it was so, that all that saw it said, There was no such deed done nor seen from the day that the children of Israel came up out of the land of Egypt unto this day: consider of it, take advice, and speak your minds.*

Bluntly, this was worse than what happened at the destruction of Sodom and Gomorrah. It was so bad that the writer said, *There was no such deed done nor seen from the day that the children of Israel came up out of the land of Egypt unto this day: consider of it, take advice, and speak your minds.*

And this is how bad God saw things in Israel when He looked at them in Hosea's day. And because they had gotten as bad or worse than Gibeah, God said, *therefore he will remember their iniquity, he will visit their sins.*

Judgment was coming, and the deadline for repentance was already passed.

Hosea 9:10 *I found Israel like grapes in the wilderness; I saw your fathers as the firstripe in the fig tree at her first time: but they went to Baalpeor, and separated themselves unto that shame; and their abominations were according as they loved.*

God here goes back into Israel's past once again, back well before Gibeah, back to the time when He first chose her to build a nation. In those days, He regarded her to be like the choicest grapes found in the wilderness and the first and best figs on the tree. They were His prized fruit—that which He loved best.

But. With Israel, there always seemed to be a but. *But they went to Baalpeor, and separated themselves unto that shame.* This goes all the way back to Numbers 25:

Numbers 25:1 *And Israel abode in Shittim, and the people began to commit whoredom with the daughters of Moab.* **2** *And they called the people unto the sacrifices of their gods: and the people did eat, and bowed down to their gods.* **3** *And Israel joined himself unto Baalpeor: and the anger of the LORD was kindled against Israel.* **4** *And the LORD said unto Moses, Take all the heads of the people, and hang them up before the LORD against the sun, that the fierce anger of the LORD may be turned away from Israel.* **5** *And Moses said unto the judges of Israel, Slay ye every one his men that were joined unto Baalpeor.*

God said of this here in Hosea 9:10 that they *separated themselves unto that shame; and their abominations were according as they loved.* They were supposed to be separated to Jehovah from idols. Instead, they separated themselves from Jehovah to Baalpeor. This was a Moabite devil that required young women to serve as his temple prostitutes. And yet, they had no problem with this because *their abominations were according as they loved.* In other words, whatever they "loved," they did, no matter how filthy and abominable.

Hosea 9:11 *As for Ephraim, their glory shall fly away like a bird, from the birth, and from the womb, and from the* *conception.* **12** *Though they bring up their children, yet will I bereave them, that there shall not be a man left: yea, woe also to them when I depart from them!*

Hosea has previously mentioned the judgment of a declining population. He does so again in these verses, both of which go together to make up one main thought.

The glory spoken of in verse eleven is the children spoken of in verse twelve. These verses describe the wholesale death of the next generation at four particular stages. Many would die during the birthing process. Many others would die in the womb. Others would die right at the point of conception, with their parents never having even become aware of them. Others, though, would be "brought up" only to have God bereave those parents of them until an entire generation was gone, and aging parents were having to start over and hope for the best out of declining virility and decaying wombs. And far from that being the end of the calamity, God added, *yea, woe also to them when I depart from them!*

They would lose their people and their God all at once.

Hosea 9:13 *Ephraim, as I saw Tyrus, is planted in a pleasant place: but Ephraim shall bring forth his children to the murderer.*

Both Tyre on the seaside and Israel with her mountains and rivers and seas and lakes were in beautiful, pleasant locations. In spite of that, Ephraim, Israel, would *bring forth his children to the murderer*. Assyria would be her midwife – a midwife there to deliver the children so that she could murder them in front of an anguished mother's eyes.

Hosea 9:14 *Give them, O LORD: what wilt thou give? give them a miscarrying womb and dry breasts.*

God has been speaking; Hosea now interjects and speaks to God. He has heard God's words of all the death and destruction that will come to young Jewish boys and girls at the hands of Assyria. And in light of that, he prays for the only mercy he can think of; he prays for his people to become barren instead, unable to carry children to full term, and therefore have breasts that are ever dry.

When that is mercy, the judgment coming is dire indeed.

Hosea 9:15 *All their wickedness is in Gilgal: for there I hated them: for the wickedness of their doings I will drive them out of mine house, I will love them no more: all their princes are revolters.*

When we covered Hosea 4, Gilgal was mentioned, and here is what I said there:

> "Gilgal was pretty famous in Jewish history. It is the place where the covenant of circumcision was renewed in Joshua 5 after all the years of the wilderness wanderings. It, therefore, pictured the rolling away of the sin of a nation. Based on that, it would seem like a perfect place for Judah to go if they really wanted to get right with God and not follow in the sinful footsteps of Israel.
>
> "But many years after that positive scene in Gilgal, it became a hotbed of idolatry under Jeroboam II. In Hosea 9:15, God will say, 'All their wickedness is in Gilgal.' " (103)

We are now at that point. Adam Clarke said of this, "Though we are not directly informed of the fact, yet we have reason to believe they had been guilty of some scandalous practices of idolatry in Gilgal." (Clarke, 642)

Clearly, they had. God saw in Gilgal a concentration of all of the wickedness in the land. Whatever idolatry could be found anywhere was found there. It was their "Superstore of Idolatry." So God now says of Gilgal, *for there I hated them: for the wickedness of their doings I will drive them out of mine house, I will love them no more: all their princes are revolters.*

Note, please, that God's hatred was not based on "election" or "predestination." It was based entirely on the wickedness of their doings. And because of how deep that wickedness was, God determined to drive them out of His house, meaning out of the Promised Land. He determined to love them no more, because all of their princes, their leaders, were revolters, meaning intentionally stubborn and rebellious against God.

But what are we to make of the fact that God would love them no more, especially in light of what He will say in the last chapter of the book? Here is what He will say there:

Hosea 14:4 *I will heal their backsliding,* ***I will love them freely****: for mine anger is turned away from him.*

In chapter nine, He promises to love them no more. In chapter fourteen, He promises to love them freely. So, which one is correct, and is there a contradiction in Scripture?

The answers, in order, are "both" and "certainly not."

This is not hard at all to unravel. The generation that was being given over to destruction at the hands of Assyria would never be loved by God again. But a future generation, willing to be different than those who came before them, would be loved freely. God would cast a *generation* away, but He would not cast *His people* away; the promises to Abraham would and will forever stand sure.

Hosea 9:16 *Ephraim is smitten, their root is dried up, they shall bear no fruit: yea, though they bring forth, yet will I slay even the beloved fruit of their womb.*

Adam Clarke really gets the sense of this verse. He describes it this way:

> "[Ephraim is smitten] The thing being determined, it is considered as already done. [Their root is dried up] They shall never more be a kingdom. And they never had any political

form from their captivity by the Assyrians to the present day." (Clarke, 643)

The present day, for him when he published those words, was 1828. If he could have lived another 120 years, he would have seen the prophecy of Ezekiel 37 fulfilled, as Israel became a nation once more. But even then, they were not and are not a kingdom. They will not be a kingdom again until the Millennial Reign of Christ. For 3,000 or so years, they have lost one of their highest privileges.

What a high price to pay for portable gods and a few moments of illicit fun! And it is especially high because the way God accomplished it, as stated in the last part of the verse, is, *yet will I slay even the beloved fruit of their womb.* This is yet another promise that God would destroy a generation of their young, those who would have had the most power to turn their tide for the better.

Hosea 9:17 *My God will cast them away, because they did not hearken unto him: and they shall be wanderers among the nations.*

There is a dual fulfillment in these words—and both are dramatic. Once sent into Assyria, history records no wholesale return of the Northern Kingdom Jews to the land. Handfuls doubtless trickled back into the land through the years, but for the most part, they dispersed and disappeared among the Gentile nations of the world.

Those from the Southern Kingdom, Judah, did return in large numbers. And they, along with the small remnant left behind by the Assyrians and the few that trickled back in through the years, made up the nation as it was in the days of Jesus and in the days of Paul.

But in A.D. 136, they were banished from the land. And for the better part of 1,800 years, they were indeed *wanderers among the nations*. Nations like Spain. Nations like Germany. Nations that despised and determined to destroy them. It would not be until 1948 that they once again had their own land. And yet, even now, even in possession of a homeland, they are still largely wanderers among the nations. As of 2023, out of approximately fifteen million Jews worldwide, only about seven million of them live in Israel. The other eight million live all over the place.

This would have been unthinkable in Hosea's day.

But the unthinkable becomes the inevitable when God's people turn their backs on Him.

Chapter Thirteen
The Dangers of a Divided Heart

Hosea 10:1 *Israel is an empty vine, he bringeth forth fruit unto himself: according to the multitude of his fruit he hath increased the altars; according to the goodness of his land they have made goodly images.* **2** *Their heart is divided; now shall they be found faulty: he shall break down their altars, he shall spoil their images.* **3** *For now they shall say, We have no king, because we feared not the LORD; what then should a king do to us?* **4** *They have spoken words, swearing falsely in making a covenant: thus judgment springeth up as hemlock in the furrows of the field.* **5** *The inhabitants of Samaria shall fear because of the calves of Bethaven: for the people thereof shall mourn over it, and the priests thereof that rejoiced on it, for the glory thereof, because it is departed from it.* **6** *It shall be also carried unto Assyria for a present to king Jareb: Ephraim shall receive shame, and Israel shall be ashamed of his own counsel.* **7** *As for Samaria, her king is cut off as the foam upon the water.* **8** *The high places also of Aven, the sin of Israel, shall be destroyed: the thorn and the thistle shall come up on their altars; and they shall say to the mountains, Cover us; and to the hills, Fall on us.* **9** *O Israel, thou hast sinned from the days of Gibeah: there they stood: the battle in Gibeah against the children of iniquity did not overtake them.* **10** *It is in my desire that I should chastise them; and the people shall be gathered against them, when they* *shall bind themselves in their two furrows.* **11** *And Ephraim is as an heifer that is taught, and loveth to tread out the corn; but I passed over upon her fair neck: I will make Ephraim to ride; Judah shall plow, and Jacob shall break his clods.* **12** *Sow to yourselves in righteousness, reap in mercy; break up your fallow ground: for it is time to seek the LORD, till he come and rain righteousness upon you.* **13** *Ye have plowed wickedness, ye have reaped iniquity; ye have eaten the fruit of lies: because thou didst trust in thy way, in the multitude of thy mighty men.* **14** *Therefore shall a tumult arise among thy people, and all thy fortresses shall be spoiled, as Shalman spoiled Betharbel in the day of battle: the mother was dashed in pieces upon her children.* **15** *So shall Bethel do unto you because of your great wickedness: in a morning shall the king of Israel utterly be cut off.*

Hosea 9 ended with the most ominous and impactful words: because of her continued rebellion, God's people we going to become wanderers among the nations. They were going to lose their homeland and be scattered among the Gentiles. And now in chapter ten we will find that the underlying problem was something that would be a bit surprising to many.

It was not that they had a departed heart; it was that they had a divided heart.

A profound division

Hosea 10:1 *Israel is an empty vine, he bringeth forth fruit unto himself: according to the multitude of his fruit he hath increased the altars; according to the goodness of his land they have made goodly images.*

The picture that God through Hosea begins to draw here is of a grapevine in a rather unique condition. This vine, Israel, is empty. And the reason it is empty is because it has brought forth fruit unto itself. In other words, the fruit that it was to bear for its master, Jehovah God, has instead been lavished up unto itself.

What an odd picture that presents! And that oddity is intentional; it is designed to make us realize how ludicrous the behavior of Israel had become. No grapevine would ever pluck its own ripe fruit and hold onto it for its own purposes, hiding it from its owner. But that is exactly what Israel was doing to God. And she had a specific purpose for so doing:

...according to the multitude of his fruit he hath increased the altars; according to the goodness of his land they have made goodly images.

The accusation that God was making against Israel in these words is that the more prosperous they became, the more idolatrous altars they built with that prosperity. The more wealthy their land became, the more elaborate, ornate, and expensive their idols became. They were taking the blessings of God and bestowing them on the devil himself.

And that makes the words of the next verse all the more shocking:

Hosea 10:2 *<u>Their heart is divided</u>; now shall they be found faulty: he shall break down their altars, he shall spoil their images.*

Israel was a land full of people who were using their wealth to build altars and idols to false gods. But, far from completely forsaking Jehovah, they were attempting to do the most illogical thing, taking Him as part of their pantheon of gods along with all of their created trinkets. And this was by no means a one-time thing for them:

1 Kings 18:21 *And Elijah came unto all the people, and said, How long halt ye between two opinions? if the LORD be God, follow him: but if Baal, then follow him. And the people answered him not a word.*

Elijah was describing the same thing Hosea was. The people were trying to follow Baal and Jehovah at the same time,

Jehovah and other false gods at the same time. They were halting between two opinions; they had a divided heart, and that logical absurdity seemed not to bother them in the least.

But it did bother God. Look again what He said after making that accusation at the beginning of verse ten, *now shall they be found faulty: he shall break down their altars, he shall spoil their images.*

God did not find them to be tolerant or contemplative or open-minded in this matter; He found them to be faulty. That word means to be guilty of a trespass. God regarded them as sinful for their divided heart. And He determined to break down their altars and spoil their images. He determined to intentionally wreck and humiliate all religion that was not His own.

He was clearly pretty serious about being regarded as the only one.

A people without leadership

Hosea 10:3 *For now they shall say, We have no king, because we feared not the LORD; what then should a king do to us?*

Looking ahead both to their immediate future and to their distant future, God warned Israel that there was going to come a day when they looked around in anguish and said the frightening words, *We have no king, because we feared not the LORD.* Worse still, they would follow that up with, *what then should a king do to us?* That was their way of saying, "We have no king, but even if we did, as bad off as we are, what good would it do us?"

After Jeroboam II died, his son was kept from the throne for roughly nine years due to civil strife. Later on down the line, the kingdom ceased entirely, along with the line of the kings. They rejected God's leadership, and God responded by removing their human leadership. To be a nation without a king in those days spelled certain destruction, and they knew it, and they experienced it.

Hosea 10:4 *They have spoken words, swearing falsely in making a covenant: thus judgment springeth up as hemlock in the furrows of the field.*

There is a bit of debate over the covenant referenced in this verse. God accused them of swearing to a covenant while knowing good and well they were lying and had no intention of keeping it. Some regard this as a covenant they made with the LORD, a covenant to obey and follow Him. Others view it as referring to the covenant they made with Shalmaneser of Assyria, which they violated in 2 Kings 7:14 by turning to So, the king of Egypt. And the truth is, both of those things fit the context of the accusation, and both are likely being referred to at once. And because of their treachery, God said, *thus judgment springeth up as hemlock in the furrows of the field.*

He has already utilized the agricultural picture of vines, and now He is using a different agricultural picture of crops in the field. Spiritually, they were hoping to grow things like wheat and barley, but were instead, as punishment for their treachery, seeing hemlock spring up in the furrows of the field. They were trying to grow that which would sustain themselves and their livestock, but their fields were instead producing weeds of deadly poison.

A life of dishonesty and covenant breaking always eventually goes that direction.

Hosea 10:5 *The inhabitants of Samaria shall fear because of the calves of Bethaven: for the people thereof shall mourn over it, and the priests thereof that rejoiced on it, for the glory thereof, because it is departed from it.*

Throughout the book of Hosea, the primary charge of idolatry that God leveled against the people was the golden calf worship that had plagued them since the days of the divided kingdom began. When Jeroboam took the ten tribes of the north, he feared that if the people of his new kingdom continued to go south to Jerusalem to worship, they would eventually return to Rehoboam and the Southern Kingdom. So he set up a golden calf in Bethel and another in Dan so that no matter where you were in the northern territory, you would be nearer to a convenient place of idolatrous worship than the one established place for true worship.

All these long years later, under Jeroboam II, those calves were still plaguing Samaria and all of the Northern Kingdom.

As God, through Hosea, began to speak of them again here, He used a biting bit of sarcasm. All throughout the Old Testament, the word used for calves was *egal*. It is a masculine form word that signifies a bull. But in this one single instance in the Old Testament, the feminine word *eglah* is used, which to them meant *a heifer*.

God was calling their prized bull a cow.

Remember that the next time someone tells you that Christians are to be concerned about people's feelings above all else. *Needlessly* offensive is a sin, but based on all of the divine and prophetic examples of Scripture, *never* offensive is a far bigger sin.

God said that *the inhabitants of Samaria shall fear because of the calves of Bethaven: for the people thereof shall mourn over it, and the priests thereof that rejoiced on it, for the glory thereof, because it is departed from it.* And the next verse explains exactly what He means by this:

Hosea 10:6 *It shall be also carried unto Assyria for a present to king Jareb: Ephraim shall receive shame, and Israel shall be ashamed of his own counsel.*

When we came across a reference to King Jareb in Hosea 5:13, I pointed out that Jareb is only found twice in Scripture, both times here in the book of Hosea. And it is a nickname, not a historical name. Jareb means "an adversary." Adam Clarke observes that "It is most likely that Pul, king of Assyria, is intended, to whom Menahem, king of Israel, appears to have given one of the golden calves, to ensure his assistance." (Clarke, 644)

In any case of identity, though, the main point is that the golden calf that Israel chose to trust instead of Jehovah God was going to be put on a cart like some oversized trinket from the thrift store and carried away into a foreign land. Because of that, Ephraim (Israel) would be red-faced with embarrassment. Her counsel through the years, as mentioned here, had been for everyone to follow the golden calf and to stay detached from the worship of Jehovah in Jerusalem. That, they believed, would keep them politically strong. Instead, it resulted in their defeat and dissolution, complete with all of the shame that came with that defeat and dissolution.

Hosea 10:7 *As for Samaria, her king is cut off as the foam upon the water.*

This is the second mention of a thrice repeated dark promise in Hosea 10. Here are those three mentions put together:

Hosea 10:3 *For now they shall say, We have no king, because we feared not the LORD; what then should a king do to us?*

Hosea 10:7 *As for Samaria, her king is cut off as the foam upon the water.*

Hosea 10:15 *So shall Bethel do unto you because of your great wickedness: in a morning shall the king of Israel utterly be cut off.*

It is not hard to figure out who the last person in the kingdom was who would ever want to hear those words: the king himself. And yet, it all came to pass exactly as God said that it would, including His promise in verse seven that her king would be cut off as the foam upon the water.

Let me give you the eloquent words of three different commentators describing this cutting off of the king in verse seven:

Adam Clarke: "As lightly as a puff of wind blows off the foam that is formed below by a fall of water, so shall the kings of Israel be cut off." (Clarke, 644)

Jamieson, Faussett, and Brown: "As the foam, though seeming to be eminent raised on the top of the water, yet has no solidity, such is the throne of Samaria." (Jamieson, 493)

Charles Spurgeon: "He floated aloft like a bubble, and was destroyed as readily." (Linder: Spurgeon)

This is not how any king would ever want to be regarded, but it was an accurate picture of the king of Samaria. And the king and kingdom did indeed fall just as God in His omniscience said that they would.

Hosea 10:8 *The high places also of Aven, the sin of Israel, shall be destroyed: the thorn and the thistle shall come up on their altars; and they shall say to the mountains, Cover us; and to the hills, Fall on us.*

We now come to what seems to be the mention of a new place in the text but which is, in reality, not a new mention at all. Aven, mentioned here by that name for the first time in Hosea, is seen only three places in the Bible. We find it here, we find it in Ezekiel 30:17, and we find it in Amos 1:5. And the key to understanding it is to realize that it is a nickname of a nickname, much like William becomes Will which becomes Bill.

So, of what is it a nickname? If you have been paying attention as we have gone through the book of Hosea, you probably already know. It is a shortened form of Bethaven (Beth-**Aven**) which is used in Hosea as a euphemism for Bethel. The high places also of Aven, Bethel, where the sin of Israel (the golden calf) was, would be destroyed. Thus, in the absence of worshippers or an object of worship, their ruined altars would have the thorns and the thistles encroach and ultimately cover them, burying them in the darkness they so richly deserved.

At that point, they, meaning the worshippers who had seen their world fall apart in front of them, would cry out for the mountains to cover them and the hills to fall on them, wishing rather to be buried by an unspeakable landslide than to be tortured and killed or carried into a faraway land.

A promised chastisement

Hosea 10:9 *O Israel, thou hast sinned from the days of Gibeah: there they stood: the battle in Gibeah against the children of iniquity did not overtake them.*

This is now the second time in the book of Hosea that we find a reference to Gibeah and the horrible sin that took place in Judges 20. We covered that all in Hosea 9:9, the rape of the concubine and the bloody scene that followed.

As God references that sin yet again here, He says that Israel has sinned from the days of Gibeah.

We need to take a few moments and work our way through that statement.

To begin with, it does not mean that that is where they as a people began sinning. The children of Israel as a whole began sinning many generations before the period of the Judges. It also does not mean that that is where the Northern Kingdom began sinning since the Northern Kingdom did not yet exist as a separate entity.

By the words He used here and the reference that He made, God was going back to the darkest point in their history and pointing out that they had not gotten any better from that day. In fact, in a rather crucial way, they had gotten worse. The last half of the verse says, *there they stood: the battle in Gibeah against the children of iniquity did not overtake them.*

Let's put some names and descriptions with those pronouns to help you understand what God was saying:

Hosea 10:9 *O Israel, thou hast sinned from the days of Gibeah: there they* [Benjamin in their wickedness] *stood: the battle in Gibeah against the children of iniquity did not overtake them* [six hundred Benjamites survived].

Here is what all of that means. After the tribe of Benjamin engaged in the most horrific wickedness, the other tribes gathered against them to destroy them. Far from repenting, though, Benjamin fought back and fought back hard. In the end, six hundred of them survived – a tiny number that allowed the tribe itself to survive. And they survived as children of iniquity, not as children who were chastised and repented. Since that day, though, rather than learning from their error, the rest of Israel adopted their error. We have already repeatedly seen in the book of Hosea the constant tie in between idolatry and the vilest of sexual sin and even much bloodshed.

The errors of others that they should have learned from instead became a pattern of life for an entire nation. Little wonder, then, that God would, this time around, take the rod of judgment in His own hand rather than leave it to His people:

Hosea 10:10 *It is in my desire that I should chastise them; and the people shall be gathered against them, when they shall bind themselves in their two furrows.*

The flowing words *It is in my desire that I should chastise them,* put in more modern vernacular, mean something like "I really want to beat the devil out of all of them."

When you have gotten God that angry with your sin, you are in very dangerous territory.

The chastisement God was going to bring against His people was that "*the people shall be gathered against them, when they shall bind themselves in their two furrows.*" People is from the word that means nations—nations like Assyria and other Gentile kingdoms who would ravage them. They, Israel, would bind themselves into two furrows, a euphemism for two columns of defense, but it would all be to no avail against their enemies.

Hosea 10:11 *And Ephraim is as an heifer that is taught, and loveth to tread out the corn; but I passed over upon her fair neck: I will make Ephraim to ride; Judah shall plow, and Jacob shall break his clods.*

Even the modern American mind will quickly see many agricultural terms and descriptions in this verse. The first one given is of Ephraim as a heifer that is taught and loves to tread out the corn. This is a picture of an animal that has been tamed, brought inside, and has a relatively easy life walking in a circle, treading out the corn. Deuteronomy 25:4 said of this situation, *Thou shalt not muzzle the ox when he treadeth out the corn.* So God's people in this picture were fat and flourishing and did not much break a sweat—and they liked it that way.

But the next thing we read gives us the second picture in this series, *but I passed over upon her fair neck.* This is a phrase that is used when a master rushes upon an animal and hastily throws a yoke on its neck and shoulders. In other words, God was about to put His people to much more rigorous service; their life of ease was coming to an end whether they liked it or not.

The third phrase and the third picture is found in the words *I will make Ephraim to ride.* This paints the picture of an animal that had either a heavy load or a heavy rider, or even both, put upon its back to carry. And in this case, the destination of this ride would be Assyria.

The final phrase and picture is found in the words *Judah shall plow, and Jacob shall break his clods.* And this picture springs out of the first three. Ephraim, Israel, had for many long years put their relatives of the Southern Kingdom of Judah to tribute and service. They had been forced to plow the ground and break the clods for their masters in the north. But now, in their absence, the Southern Kingdom, Jacob/Judah, would plow and work the fields for her own benefit, not for the benefit of others.

Israel's chastisement would be Judah's deliverance.

A plan for renewal

Hosea 10:12 *Sow to yourselves in righteousness, reap in mercy; break up your fallow ground: for it is time to seek the LORD, till he come and rain righteousness upon you.*

It is clear that God, through Hosea, is still utilizing agricultural pictures in verse twelve. The subject matter, though, has shifted from what they currently are to the potential of what could be. They are going to be judged; that much has long been settled in time and in the text. But just like there is hope for a worthless field at some point in the future, there is hope for Israel as well. Because of that, they are to sow to themselves in righteousness. They have long planted seeds that have only grown poisonous crops; they are now to sow the seeds of righteousness that will eventually grow pleasant crops instead. They have reaped in injustice, taking that which did not belong to them from people who were too weak to stop them. They are now to reap in mercy, taking only that which is their due and, in necessary cases, simply forgiving the debt outright.

The last half of the verse presents some of the most profound words in Scripture, *break up your fallow ground: for it is time to seek the LORD, till he come and rain righteousness upon you.*

Fallow ground was hard, untilled ground. And this picture was of the heart of God's people, not their property. God expected them to drop a plow deep into their hardened hearts and break up their stony souls so that God could do a work within them again. The status quo would no longer be acceptable; it was time for them to truly seek the LORD, and to do so until He chose to come and rain righteousness upon them, causing good crops once again to grow within them.

It would be hard to imagine a more appropriate picture for much of Christendom today. We wonder why it seems only weeds are growing within us at best when the fault is in our own hardened and untilled hearts.

A painful reality

Hosea 10:13 *Ye have plowed wickedness, ye have reaped iniquity; ye have eaten the fruit of lies: because thou didst trust in thy way, in the multitude of thy mighty men.*

This is the last verse in the agricultural series of pictures God has been painting. And it ties directly back to the verse before it. Verse twelve began with sowing and reaping; verse thirteen begins with plowing and reaping.

God rightfully accused His people of plowing wickedness, the diametrical opposite of the sowing in righteousness He required of them one verse earlier. He accused them of reaping iniquity, the diametrical opposite of the reaping in mercy that He required of them one verse earlier. And as a summary of all of that, He ends the verse by saying *ye have eaten the fruit of lies: because thou didst trust in thy way, in the multitude of thy mighty men.*

In modern vernacular, they were getting what they got by lies and deceit because they were overconfident due to the multitude of their mighty men. Their "gang" led them to the foolish idea that no one and nothing could ever take them down.

They were wrong:

Hosea 10:14 *Therefore shall a tumult arise among thy people, and all thy fortresses shall be spoiled, as Shalman spoiled Betharbel in the day of battle: the mother was dashed in pieces upon her children.*

Therefore, because they trusted in their many mighty men and oppressed those who could not stand against them, God was going to send a tumult [a crashing, a roaring] among them, and all their fortresses would fall and be spoiled. As a present-day reminder of that, He further said, *as Shalman spoiled Betharbel in the day of battle: the mother was dashed in pieces upon her children.*

Shalman is a shortened form of Shalmaneser, the king of Assyria, which we have already discussed at some length. When he took the city of Betharbel, it was clearly a scene of great brutality, with neither mother nor children being spared so much as an ounce of it. Israel obviously knew about this, or God would not have had Hosea reference it for them here.

And there was a very definite point for Him bringing it up:

Hosea 10:15 *So shall Bethel do unto you because of your great wickedness: in a morning shall the king of Israel utterly be cut off.*

Their idolatry in Bethel would lead to them being ravaged by Assyria just as brutally as Betharbel was. In a single morning, the king himself would be cut off.

The kingdom was dying. They were about to lose everything they held dear in the most horrific fashion.

These are the dangers of a divided heart.

Chapter Fourteen
The Turning of the Tide

Hosea 11:1 *When Israel was a child, then I loved him, and called my son out of Egypt.* **2** *As they called them, so they went from them: they sacrificed unto Baalim, and burned incense to graven images.* **3** *I taught Ephraim also to go, taking them by their arms; but they knew not that I healed them.* **4** *I drew them with cords of a man, with bands of love: and I was to them as they that take off the yoke on their jaws, and I laid meat unto them.* **5** *He shall not return into the land of Egypt, but the Assyrian shall be his king, because they refused to return.* **6** *And the sword shall abide on his cities, and shall consume his branches, and devour them, because of their own counsels.* **7** *And my people are bent to backsliding from me: though they called them to the most High, none at all would exalt him.* **8** *How shall I give thee up, Ephraim? how shall I deliver thee, Israel? how shall I make thee as Admah? how shall I set thee as Zeboim? mine heart is turned within me, my repentings are kindled together.* **9** *I will not execute the fierceness of mine anger, I will not return to destroy Ephraim: for I am God, and not man; the Holy One in the midst of thee: and I will not enter into the city.* **10** *They shall walk after the LORD: he shall roar like a lion: when he shall roar, then the children shall tremble from the west.* **11** *They shall tremble as a bird out of Egypt, and as a dove out of the land of Assyria: and I will place them in their houses,* *saith the LORD.* **12** *Ephraim compasseth me about with lies, and the house of Israel with deceit: but Judah yet ruleth with God, and is faithful with the saints.*

In Hosea 10, God castigated Israel for her divided heart. As ever, she was intent on having her Jehovah—and at the same time, having all of her created gods as well. God, the real God, assured her that this would never be acceptable in His sight, and that there would be a price to pay.

Among other things, her king would be cut off; her nation would fail and be dispersed. So for several chapters, it has been almost entirely bad news, and now that news was about as bad as it gets.

But the one thing consistent about the tide is that it always eventually turns; that is the way God designed it.

A reminder and a prophecy

Hosea 11:1 *When Israel was a child, then I loved him, and called my son out of Egypt.*

Israel, a people that was not at all enjoying what they were hearing from Hosea, was now being taken back in time to the very beginning of their nation, and to the words of Moses. The words Hosea references here had their initial public hearing in the court of Pharoah:

Exodus 4:22 *And thou shalt say unto Pharaoh, Thus saith the LORD, Israel is my son, even my firstborn:* **23** *And I say unto thee, Let my son go, that he may serve me: and if thou refuse to let him go, behold, I will slay thy son, even thy firstborn.*

For Israel in Hosea's day, this was a very encouraging reminder. Would they go into captivity in Assyria? Yes; that much was firmly settled. But had God already called them out of bondage before? Absolutely. In fact, that is how they became an independent nation to begin with. When they were a child, meaning a very young people rather than an old, long established nation, God loved them and brought them out of Egypt and into the Promised Land. This, therefore, was an assurance that the God who brought them out of their past bondage could certainly do so in their coming bondage.

But it was also something more than a reminder—it was a prophecy:

Matthew 2:13 *And when they were departed, behold, the angel of the Lord appeareth to Joseph in a dream, saying, Arise, and take the young child and his mother, and flee into Egypt, and be thou there until I bring thee word: for Herod will seek the young child to destroy him.* **14** *When he arose, he took the young child and his mother by night, and departed into Egypt:* **15** *And was there until the death of Herod: that it might be fulfilled which was spoken of the Lord by the prophet, saying, Out of Egypt have I called my son.*

Many things written in the Old Testament were clearly meant to be both proclamation and prophecy. And the New Testament, written by the same God who authored the Old Testament, makes those prophetical applications clear. Whether anyone in Hosea's day understood it to be a prophecy of the Messiah/Christ child is irrelevant; it was a prophecy of Him, and God made that clear to Matthew.

God called His firstborn national son, Israel, out of Egypt and into the Promised Land. God called His firstborn and only begotten Son, Jesus, out of Egypt and back into the Promised Land. Looking back, Matthew was able to see and understand that, all those long years earlier, God was painting pictures of what He was going to do, and that those pictures were now finished and ready to be displayed to the world.

A rejection and a price

Hosea 11:2 *As they called them, so they went from them: they sacrificed unto Baalim, and burned incense to graven images.*

Considering that the context of this verse is Israel being called out of Egypt and becoming a nation, a nation expected to follow only Jehovah God, the theys and thems of this verse are easy to figure out. They, the prophets starting with Moses and Aaron and coming all the way down the line to Hosea himself, called them, the Children of Israel, to love and serve only Jehovah God. But the more they called them, the more they went from them and served Baalim and a host of other graven images. They very early on started this constant habit of rejecting the God who gave them birth as a nation.

But they did not just refuse the pleading of their prophets:

Hosea 11:3 *I taught Ephraim also to go, taking them by their arms; but they knew not that I healed them.*

This was God speaking; He is the "I" in this verse. So not only did the prophets try to get the people to do right, God Himself took time to teach Ephraim, put here again for Israel; He took them by their arms.

The wording used here is incredibly picturesque. It is the picture of a mother helping her child to learn to walk. She holds him up, putting her hands under his arms, and helps to support him as he gets his balance and learns to put one foot in front of the other. (Clarke, 646)

This is what God did for Israel as He brought them out of Egypt and taught them how to live and to serve Him! And all of this is what makes the end of the verse such a tragedy, *but they knew not that I healed them.*

God was teaching them how to walk right so that they could grow up and be strong and healthy; all they saw, though, were restrictions in those loving hands. They longed to run and to run where it was harmful to go, and they chafed at any prophet and even at God Himself when they were prohibited.

Hosea 11:4 *I drew them with cords of a man, with bands of love: and I was to them as they that take off the yoke on their jaws, and I laid meat unto them.*

As He has done so often in the last few chapters, God once again uses an agricultural reference to paint a picture of what He had done and was doing.

This particular picture is in three parts. In the first, He says, *"I drew them with cords of a man, with bands of love."*

What He is describing is the difference between how an animal would be led and how a young and precious child would be led. An animal, a mere beast of burden, would be led by having a stout rope tied to it so that it could be pulled and turned at will. But with a child, the practice was for a parent to hold onto one end of a soft cord and allow the child to hold onto the other end of it so that the child could both be led and also feel like he had some support to steady him as he learned to walk. This is what is meant by the cords of a man, the bands of love.

The second part of the picture is *and I was to them as they that take off the yoke on their jaws.* This was a picture of how a caring master would not always leave his animal yoked and with a bit in his mouth. He made sure to remove it as needed for the animal's comfort and benefit.

The third part of the picture is *and I laid meat unto them.* This was the picture of how, after taking those things off of the animal, the caring master would set food in front of the animal, making sure its needs were met.

God was reminding Israel that, though they were rightfully expected to serve Him, He was very kind to them, and they had things good.

Hosea 11:5 *He shall not return into the land of Egypt, but the Assyrian shall be his king, because they refused to return.*

Was God good to Israel? Yes, certainly. But did Israel use that goodness as an occasion to seek after the God of that goodness? No. Instead, as Hosea 7:11 proclaimed, they had sought after Egypt instead. In 2 Kings 17:4, they had sought refuge in Egypt against Assyria.

But God here, as elsewhere, made it clear that such plan was doomed to fail. They would not get to independently return into Egypt as a people; instead, they would mostly go into captivity in Assyria because they refused to return to God. And this was going to have a devastating impact on their land:

Hosea 11:6 *And the sword shall abide on his cities, and shall consume his branches, and devour them, because of their own counsels.*

It was the sword that they sought to avoid by refusing to return to God and following their own counsels.

It was the sword that they received by refusing to return to God and following their own counsels. They ended up with external and internal conflict from the time of Jeroboam II. His son, Zechariah, reigned for twelve years, in conflict the entire time, and he was finally murdered by Shallum. Shallum reigned for just one month and was slain by Menahem. Pekahiah succeeded his father, Menahem, reigned just two years, and was killed by Pekah, son of Remaliah. Pekah invaded Judah, was defeated, and the tribes of Reuben, Gad, Naphtali, and the half-tribe of Manasseh were carried away captive by the Assyrian king. Shortly after that, Hoshea, son of Elah, assassinated Pekah and took the kingdom. But he did this with the assistance of Shalmaneser, who laid a heavy tribute on him for that assistance. Trying to get free from that, he sought for help from the king of Egypt. When Shalmaneser found that out, he came against Samaria, and after a three-year siege took and destroyed it.

It happened exactly as God said it would; the sword rested on their cities until everything was ruined. (Clarke, 646)

A rebellion and a passing

Hosea 11:7 *And my people are bent to backsliding from me: though they called them to the most High, none at all would exalt him.*

Why would Israel suffer such an obviously inevitable fate as described in verse six? You just read the answer here in verse seven: they were bent to backsliding from God. They did not just slowly, accidentally, through the course of long years end up backslidden. This was not a matter of something happening so subtly as to not be noticed. They were *bent* to backsliding; this was an intentional, rebellious choice. And though they, meaning the prophets, called them to the Most High, all of them, the people, refused to exalt Him; their non-praising lips were as intentional as their backsliding lives. They were offered the right path, and they intentionally passed it by.

A return and a promise

Hosea 11:8 *How shall I give thee up, Ephraim? how shall I deliver thee, Israel? how shall I make thee as Admah? how shall I set thee as Zeboim? mine heart is turned within me, my repentings are kindled together.*

We have been calling this study *Love When It Matters Most,* and we are seeing again why that is the case. Hosea determined to judge and chasten Gomer—he also chose to love and restore her at her lowest moment, when she seemed to be of no more worth. God determined to judge and chasten Israel— He also chose to love and restore her at her lowest moment, when she seemed to be of no more worth.

In the most emotional of terms, the God who created facts and figures, logic and mathematics, said, *How shall I give thee up, Ephraim? how shall I deliver thee* [deliver over to the enemy], *Israel?* The kind and loving heart of God simply could not bear to let His people go, though they unquestionably deserved it. He followed those questions of the heart with, *how shall I make thee as Admah? how shall I set thee as Zeboim?*

Admah and Zeboim may perhaps not be familiar to you. But you do know the other two famous cities that they were destroyed along with:

Deuteronomy 29:23 *And that the whole land thereof is brimstone, and salt, and burning, that it is not sown, nor beareth, nor any grass groweth therein, like the overthrow of Sodom, and Gomorrah, Admah, and Zeboim, which the LORD overthrew in his anger, and in his wrath:*

Admah and Zeboim were cities in the same plane as Sodom and Gomorrah, cities enmeshed in the same wickedness, cities that, just like Sodom and Gomorrah, perished in that terrible night of judgment. So, why did God not say, "How shall I make thee as Sodom? how shall I set thee as Gomorrah?" Why did He instead use the names of those two other, lesser-known cities that were destroyed along with Sodom and Gomorrah? In other places, He did refer to His people by those names. Why not here?

Because His heart was breaking for His people. The God who made us in His image and gave us emotions gave us the same emotions that He Himself has. And at this point, looking at what was about to happen to the people He loved, His mercy and compassion was rising to the top. Here is how He expressed that at the end of this verse, *mine heart is turned within me, my repentings are kindled together.*

Let those words sink in: God's heart was turned within Him. As He considered the fall, captivity, and dispersion of His people at the hands of the Assyrians, His heart was turned toward mercy, and His repentings, His changes of purposed direction, were kindled together, meaning they were heating up.

Let me put this in simple terms. God, in righteous anger, was sending His people away for the ruin of that generation and many generations to follow. But though His people deserved all of this and more, though they deserved to be utterly forsaken and forgotten, the heart of God could not do that; He loved them too much to allow His judgment to go that far. And these words, to Hosea's generation, were a promise that though they would fall, their descendants of long years into the future would one day be brought back to their land and their God.

Hosea 9:11 *I will not execute the fierceness of mine anger, I will not return to destroy Ephraim: for I am God, and not man; the Holy One in the midst of thee: and I will not enter into the city.*

Was God fiercely angry? Yes, absolutely. But He has now chosen not to execute (accomplish, bring about) the fierceness of His anger. He could return to Ephraim to destroy them, but He chooses not to do so because He is God and not man. Man never seems to back away from the fierceness of deserved anger; God does. And He backs away from the fierceness of His anger, not as "the tolerant and waffling one," as we might be inclined to think, but as *the Holy One in the midst of thee.*

What wonder, that the holiness of God is as much tied to mercy as it is to judgment! What wonder that, at His angriest, He says *and I will not enter into the city,* when His entering in at that point would have been fatal.

Hosea 11:10 *They shall walk after the LORD: he shall roar like a lion: when he shall roar, then the children shall tremble from the west.*

Hosea's people were going to fall. They would not survive to see what was spoken of here. But it would come to be, and God was already seeing it. There would come a day when the people who were bent to backsliding would instead walk after the LORD. There would come a day when He, the LORD, would roar like a lion, and the children, HIS children, would tremble from the west. But this trembling would be in anticipation, not in fear; the Lion would be calling His children home. The west, as John Wesley accurately observes, is used here as a euphemism for the ends of the earth. (Linder: John Wesley's Notes)

Has this taken place, or is it yet to take place?

Yes.

As with so many Old Testament prophecies, this one applied both to events not too far removed from their days and to events drastically removed from their days. By the time of Christ, a remnant of the people were back in the land, and things were somewhat normal. But ultimately, this looked ahead in time both to the modern-day restoration of Israel after a nearly 2000-year dispersion, and even further to God's final restoration of them in the Millennial Reign of Christ.

Hosea 11:11 *They shall tremble as a bird out of Egypt, and as a dove out of the land of Assyria: and I will place them in their houses, saith the LORD.*

Verse eleven is much more about the near fulfillment of what God has been saying than the ultimate fulfillment; it has brought things back to the area of Egypt and Assyria, not the ends of the earth. As Clarke observed, "Those of them that are in Egypt shall also be called thence, and shall speed hither as a bird. Those in Assyria shall also be called to return, and they shall flee as doves to their windows. All shall, in the fulness of time, return to their own land." (Clarke, 647)

God was going to bring His people back from hopelessness and put them in their houses.

A rottenness and a purity

Hosea 11:12 *Ephraim compasseth me about with lies, and the house of Israel with deceit: but Judah yet ruleth with God, and is faithful with the saints.*

Having looked ahead to the mercy God will extend His people and the restoration He will afford them, chapter eleven now ends with God coming back to Hosea's day and the conditions therein. The Northern Kingdom, Ephraim/Israel, was encircling God with their lies and deceit day after day. It is as if their dishonesty was swirling on the wind with God in the midst of it all.

Judah, though, the Southern Kingdom, was currently in a different and far better condition. At present, they were ruling with God and being faithful with the saints. These phrases indicate that they still had a proper monarchy and priesthood, institutions that still reflected the commandments and values of God. They were by no means perfect; the very next chapter will once again return to a bit of a castigation of them. But they had periods in which they were incredibly pleasing in God's sight, and compared to the Northern Kingdom, they were the pure ones.

Israel was going to fall. Judah was going to continue on for a while longer. But ultimately, a loving God would leave neither in their exile.

Chapter Fifteen
Shadows of the Past, Stains of the Present

Hosea 12:1 *Ephraim feedeth on wind, and followeth after the east wind: he daily increaseth lies and desolation; and they do make a covenant with the Assyrians, and oil is carried into Egypt.* **2** *The LORD hath also a controversy with Judah, and will punish Jacob according to his ways; according to his doings will he recompense him.* **3** *He took his brother by the heel in the womb, and by his strength he had power with God:* **4** *Yea, he had power over the angel, and prevailed: he wept, and made supplication unto him: he found him in Bethel, and there he spake with us;* **5** *Even the LORD God of hosts; the LORD is his memorial.* **6** *Therefore turn thou to thy God: keep mercy and judgment, and wait on thy God continually.* **7** *He is a merchant, the balances of deceit are in his hand: he loveth to oppress.* **8** *And Ephraim said, Yet I am become rich, I have found me out substance: in all my labours they shall find none iniquity in me that were sin.* **9** *And I that am the LORD thy God from the land of Egypt will yet make thee to dwell in tabernacles, as in the days of the solemn feast.* **10** *I have also spoken by the prophets, and I have multiplied visions, and used similitudes, by the ministry of the prophets.* **11** *Is there iniquity in Gilead? surely they are vanity: they sacrifice bullocks in Gilgal; yea, their altars are as heaps in the furrows of the fields.* **12** *And Jacob fled into the country of Syria, and Israel served for a wife, and for a wife he* *kept sheep.* **13** *And by a prophet the LORD brought Israel out of Egypt, and by a prophet was he preserved.* **14** *Ephraim provoked him to anger most bitterly: therefore shall he leave his blood upon him, and his reproach shall his Lord return unto him.*

In Hosea 11, God used some powerful and poignant pictures to show His tenderness toward Israel. And He also gave them glorious hope for the future; despite their past and present sins, He was going to restore them in future generations to their land and to their glory.

But as that chapter ended, God, for the time being, brought things right back around to Israel/Ephraim's present-day sin and wickedness. And that is still in focus as chapter twelve begins.

A lack of substance

Hosea 12:1 *Ephraim feedeth on wind, and followeth after the east wind: he daily increaseth lies and desolation; and they do make a covenant with the Assyrians, and oil is carried into Egypt.*

As God begins to lay more examples of disobedience to Ephraim's charge, He accuses them here of feeding on the wind and following after the east wind. And those phrases would seem obscure and difficult to understand, save for one thing: He explains them in the very next phrase. Feeding on the wind and following after the east wind is God's way of describing *he daily increaseth lies and desolation.*

Here is how all of that works together in picture form. The wind has no substance, and the east wind in Middle Eastern countries is almost always destructive rather than beneficial. Ephraim, then, was telling lies and believing his own lies, lies like "we can weasel our way out of all this by making a covenant with the Assyrians that we do not intend to keep, and then sending oil down into Egypt to bribe them to help us defeat the Assyrians."

They would eventually learn the hard way how horrible of a plan all of that was; Egypt abandoned them in their hour of greatest need, and the Assyrians absolutely wrecked them.

A look back

In the last verse of Hosea 11, God had a few positive things to say about Judah, the Southern Kingdom. But as I told you then, that was quickly going to change, and it does so here:

Hosea 12:2 *The LORD hath also a controversy with Judah, and will punish Jacob according to his ways; according to his doings will he recompense him.*

This is now the second time in the book of Hosea that God says He has a controversy with His people. The first one was back in the first verse of chapter four. Israel was mentioned there, but here it is applied to Judah, the Southern Kingdom. And just as Israel is often called by the nickname of Ephraim, one of his tribes, God here calls Judah by the name of Jacob, who was the father of the twelve tribes. And Judah/Jacob, under King Ahaz, had devolved to nearly as degraded state as Israel, even burning their own children alive in Moloch's fires (2 Chronicles 28:3).

God told the inhabitants of the Southern Kingdom that He was going to punish them according to their ways and would recompense or reward them according to their doings. And if that sounds a great deal like the law of sowing and reaping, it is because that is exactly what it is. For so very long, God's people had rested in their descent from Abraham, Isaac, and Jacob, vainly imagining that God would give them a pass on any wrongdoing because of it. But now they are being told in no uncertain terms that God will not play favorites with them; they are going to be judged because of their iniquity.

The verses that follow that promise show how egregious their fall was by reminding them of their father, Jacob.

Hosea 12:3 *He took his brother by the heel in the womb, and by his strength he had power with God:*

There is a divine ultrasound in these words on Hosea's pages. Back in the Genesis account of the birth of Jacob and Esau, we got to see what happened immediately after both of the boys were born:

Genesis 25:26 *And after that came his brother out, and his hand took hold on Esau's heel; and his name was called Jacob: and Isaac was threescore years old when she bare them.*

But here in Hosea's account, God enlightens us to the fact that this heel grabbing was taking place even in the womb! And that makes the words of Rebekah even more understandable:

Genesis 25:22 *And the children struggled together within her; and she said, If it be so, why am I thus? And she went to enquire of the LORD.*

Putting all of that together, we learn that in the womb, Jacob was grabbing the heel of Esau, and that Esau was kicking to get out of his grasp. No wonder Rebecca went to the Lord in anguish and said in so many words, "Dear God, you have to help me; it feels like a world war is going on in there!"

The words that God was reminding Judah of here in Hosea, this historical episode of Jacob grabbing Esau's heel both in the womb and on the birthing table, were designed to remind them of their privileged station before God. The common cultural expectation of the day was that the younger would serve the older. But God flipped that on its head and chose for the older to serve the younger. And the privileged station did not stop there. The last half of the verse says, *and by his strength he had power with God:*

As with everything else we have seen thus far in Hosea 12, the text is going to explain itself in very clear detail:

Hosea 12:4a *Yea, he had power over the angel, and prevailed:*

This strength with God, this power over the angel, this prevailing, winning in a battle, is found in Genesis 32:24-29. This is where Jacob, there by the brook in the middle of the night, fought with an angel that actually turned out to be God Himself in the form of an angel.

This is where they came from. Their heritage was that of a spiritual giant who did marvelously with God in spite of the deep character flaws he so often demonstrated.

And the greatness just continues on in the text:

Hosea 12:4b *...he wept, and made supplication unto him:*

We have the account of Jacob's desperate prayer in Genesis 32 when he realized that his brother Esau was on the way to kill him. Here, though, God adds the detail that he wept as he prayed those prayers. Unlike the modern children of Israel of Hosea's day whose heart was hardened and whose confidence was in their own machinations, Jacob was able to realize his own weakness and pour out a broken heart to the Lord.

The last section of verse four, along with verse five, will show us another episode in the life of Jacob, one that occurs earlier in time than the ones we have just been examining:

Hosea 12:4c *...he found him in Bethel, and there he spake with us;* **5** *Even the LORD God of hosts; the LORD is his memorial.*

These verses are an accounting of Genesis 28 where, after Jacob fled from home and stopped in Bethel to spend the night, God found him and met with him and spoke to him. And the reason the word *us* is used at the end of verse four is because when God found and spoke to Jacob that night, the future children of Israel were included in those words:

Genesis 28:13 *And, behold, the LORD stood above it, and said, I am the LORD God of Abraham thy father, and the*

*God of Isaac: the land whereon thou liest, to thee will I give it, and to **thy seed;** 14 And **thy seed** shall be as the dust of the earth, and thou shalt spread abroad to the west, and to the east, and to the north, and to the south: and in thee and in **thy seed** shall all the families of the earth be blessed. 15 And, behold, I am with thee, and will keep thee in all places whither thou goest, and will bring thee again into this land; for I will not leave thee, until I have done that which I have spoken to thee of.*

Those words of verse five, *Even the LORD God of hosts; the LORD is his memorial*, served as a reminder of what God Jacob was dealing with and the present-day role He was to be having in the lives of His people. We twice see the name Jehovah in those words, as the LORD in all capital letters always signifies. We see that He is the God of hosts, meaning the God of armies. In this self-existent God of armies is his, Jacob's memorial. In other words, the people of Hosea's day, by worshipping their idols, were wrecking their own memorial, degrading their glorious past with God.

Hosea 12:6 *Therefore turn thou to thy God: keep mercy and judgment, and wait on thy God continually.*

The history of the root of the people had been given. But it was not a mere academic exercise; there was a point to it all, a point introduced by the word *therefore* that begins verse six. *Therefore*, because God so gloriously built them as a people starting with Jacob, they were to turn to their God, keep mercy and judgment, and wait on their God continually.

John Wesley summed this list up very well, saying:

"Turn-Repent, leave idols and all sins. He [Jacob] worshipped God alone, do you so; he cast idols out of his family, do you so too; be Jacob's children herein. Mercy-Shew kindness to all who need it. Judgment-Wrong none; but with justice in dealings, in judicatures; and public offices, render to every one their due. Wait on thy

God - In public worship and private duties serve and trust God alone: let not idols have either sacrifice, prayer, praise, or trust from you; and let your hope and worship be for ever continued."
(Linder: John Wesley's Notes)

If I could paraphrase that in fewer words, it would be, "If you want the relationship with Me that Jacob had, be as devoted to Me as Jacob was, and prove it by the way you live."

If only they would have heeded that guidance; but as the next verse and those to follow will make clear, they would not do so.

Hosea 12:7 *He is a merchant, the balances of deceit are in his hand: he loveth to oppress.*

The *he* in this verse is once again referring back to Ephraim, who was the opening subject of verse one of this chapter. And when God in this verse calls him a merchant, it is not a complimentary reference. There are three main Hebrew words translated as merchant or merchants in the Old Testament. The main ones used are *cachar,* meaning one who travels to and fro in business, and *rakal,* meaning a trafficker of merchandise.

But in a tiny number of instances, three, in fact, a different word from those two main words is used, and this is one of those times. In this case, it is from the word *kenah-an*, which just so happens to be the same word that Canaanite comes from. People in those days used this word as an insult to describe people who were dishonest in their dealings. Some of you older folks know of a similar example from our modern era because of that world-famous theologian, Cher...

In 1971, she sang these words: "They'd call us gypsies, tramps, and thieves, but every night all the men would come around and lay their money down."

Gypsies is where we got the phrase "getting gypped." That phrase came from the supposed dishonest dealing of the Romani, who back then were sometimes called Gypsies. That is what God through Hosea is doing here when He uses the word for Canaanite/merchant to describe Ephraim. And the end of verse seven bears that out, saying, *the balances of deceit are in his hand: he loveth to oppress.*

Balances of deceit were balances that were rigged to be either a bit too heavy or a bit too light depending on whether one was buying or selling something. Ephraim loved this; he loved to oppress those he should have been dealing fairly with. And please remember the time period; Israel was in its second golden age financially. So when people did things like this, it was not out of desperation; it was out of pure greed. And to make it even worse, they were "spiritual" about it:

Hosea 12:8 *And Ephraim said, Yet I am become rich, I have found me out substance: in all my labours they shall find none iniquity in me that were sin.*

The prophets repeatedly called Israel/Ephraim down for their greed and dirty dealings. And yet their answer was the words of verse eight: *Yet I am become rich, I have found me out substance: in all my labours they shall find none iniquity in me that were sin.*

They used the prosperity they achieved as proof that they had done no wrong. No, it doesn't make any sense, but very little ever makes sense when coming from the lips of liars and thieves.

Ephraim had their say; now God would speak yet again:

Hosea 12:9 *And I that am the LORD thy God from the land of Egypt will yet make thee to dwell in tabernacles, as in the days of the solemn feast.*

There is a fairly even division among commentators as to whether God was promising judgment or mercy in this verse. My answer is, both the context and the then current culture of the people point to this being judgment.

The context is Ephraim being like a bunch of Canaanites: deceptive and greedy and underhanded. In that context, God reminds them that He has been their God from the land of Egypt and promises that He is going to make them dwell in tabernacles as in the days of the solemn feast, the Feast of Tabernacles. If these words had been spoken to a people doing right and seeking after God, they most assuredly would have been regarded as a blessing because when they were right with God, the Feast of Tabernacles was very precious and enjoyable to them.

But they were not truly celebrating the Feast of Tabernacles and the God who gave it anymore; they were worshipping idols. So when God told them He was going to make them dwell in tents like they used to do during the Feast of Tabernacles, this was a promise that He was going to break their prosperity and reduce them to poverty; they were going to go from homes to hovels.

Hosea 12:10 *I have also spoken by the prophets, and I have multiplied visions, and used similitudes, by the ministry of the prophets.*

Adam Clarke gives an excellent paraphrase of God's words here:

> "I have used every means, and employed every method, to instruct and save you. I have sent prophets, who spake plainly, exhorting, warning, and beseeching you to return to me. They have had Divine visions, which they have declared and interpreted. They have used similitudes, symbols, metaphors, allegories, etc., in order to fix your attention, and bring you back to your duty and interest. And, alas! all is in vain; you have not profited by my condescension." (Clarke, 649)

That is very accurate. Even Christ did much the same during His earthly ministry, sometimes speaking in riveting parables and other times in point-blank bluntness. And this, by the way, is a good thing for ministers to be able to do today.

Those who have zero variety in their speaking are limiting both themselves and their results.

Hosea 12:11 *Is there iniquity in Gilead? surely they are vanity: they sacrifice bullocks in Gilgal; yea, their altars are as heaps in the furrows of the fields.*

God mentions two geographical locations as He asks a rhetorical question about iniquity in the land. Gilead, often called Mizpeh-Gilead, was on the other side of the Jordan River to the east. Gilgal was on the western side of the Jordan. The implication, then, is that in all parts of the land, there was iniquity; it was not confined to a small pocket somewhere; it was ubiquitous.

There were three things God saw in this verse in the people of these and other locations. He saw that they were vanity, meaning empty, light, and worthless. He saw that they sacrificed bullocks, but to their idols, not to Him. He saw that they had so many idolatrous altars that they looked like rows in a field.

No wonder He was sending them into captivity!

Hosea 12:12 *And Jacob fled into the country of Syria, and Israel served for a wife, and for a wife he kept sheep.*

At first blush, it is easy to think that God has completely jumped subjects, but that is not at all the case. He has just gotten done chewing them out for all of their idolatrous altars, altars that were so numerous they seemed like rows in a field. So this reminder of Jacob as a flat-broke nobody who had to work seven years for a wife at a very menial, bottom-of-the-barrel job was designed to make them realize how good God had been to them to bring them to the Promised Land and give them a kingdom and make them wealthy. It was designed to make them ashamed for forsaking Him in favor of their handmade gods. And that line of conversation was going to continue on into the next verse:

Hosea 12:13 *And by a prophet the LORD brought Israel out of Egypt, and by a prophet was he preserved.*

This brought back to their mind the years of slavery in Egypt and the fact that God raised up Moses to deliver them from that bondage and preserve them for forty years in the wilderness.

A lingering mark

Hosea 12:14 *Ephraim provoked him to anger most bitterly: therefore shall he leave his blood upon him, and his reproach shall his Lord return unto him.*

In spite of all of God's goodness, Israel/Ephraim provoked God to anger, and not in a small way. In fact, their history, both in the wilderness wanderings and even in the Promised Land, was a continuing cycle of them doing so. And because of that, God was going to leave his, Ephraim's, blood on him, and return Israel's reproach of God right back to them.

In other words, this would be a stain that was not going to simply fade away.

And the fact that we are still talking about it 2,500 or so years later is proof that God meant what He said about it.

Chapter Sixteen
The Quickest Path to Struggleville

Hosea 13:1 *When Ephraim spake trembling, he exalted himself in Israel; but when he offended in Baal, he died.* **2** *And now they sin more and more, and have made them molten images of their silver, and idols according to their own understanding, all of it the work of the craftsmen: they say of them, Let the men that sacrifice kiss the calves.* **3** *Therefore they shall be as the morning cloud, and as the early dew that passeth away, as the chaff that is driven with the whirlwind out of the floor, and as the smoke out of the chimney.* **4** *Yet I am the LORD thy God from the land of Egypt, and thou shalt know no god but me: for there is no saviour beside me.* **5** *I did know thee in the wilderness, in the land of great drought.* **6** *According to their pasture, so were they filled; they were filled, and their heart was exalted; therefore have they forgotten me.* **7** *Therefore I will be unto them as a lion: as a leopard by the way will I observe them:* **8** *I will meet them as a bear that is bereaved of her whelps, and will rend the caul of their heart, and there will I devour them like a lion: the wild beast shall tear them.* **9** *O Israel, thou hast destroyed thyself; but in me is thine help.* **10** *I will be thy king: where is any other that may save thee in all thy cities? and thy judges of whom thou saidst, Give me a king and princes?* **11** *I gave thee a king in mine anger, and took him away in my wrath.* **12** *The iniquity of Ephraim is bound up; his sin is hid.* **13** *The sorrows* *of a travailing woman shall come upon him: he is an unwise son; for he should not stay long in the place of the breaking forth of children.* **14** *I will ransom them from the power of the grave; I will redeem them from death: O death, I will be thy plagues; O grave, I will be thy destruction: repentance shall be hid from mine eyes.* **15** *Though he be fruitful among his brethren, an east wind shall come, the wind of the LORD shall come up from the wilderness, and his spring shall become dry, and his fountain shall be dried up: he shall spoil the treasure of all pleasant vessels.* **16** *Samaria shall become desolate; for she hath rebelled against her God: they shall fall by the sword: their infants shall be dashed in pieces, and their women with child shall be ripped up.*

God spent a good bit of time in the last chapter pointing Israel back to her past to try to teach her lessons about the present, because her present was about to wreck her future. And He will begin this chapter with another nod to the past and a continued warning of what was heading their way.

A contrast between humility and pride

Hosea 13:1 *When Ephraim spake trembling, he exalted himself in Israel; but when he offended in Baal, he died.*

There is a general statement about the tribe of Ephraim's past given in this verse. There was a time when they, as a tribe, were very humble; they "spake trembling." There was no arrogance in them; whatever God wanted, they wanted. And when it was like that, Ephraim ended up being exalted in Israel, becoming one of the most prominent tribes, so much so that in later years, as we have seen repeatedly, God just called the entire Northern Kingdom by the name Ephraim.

But there came a day when they laid aside their humility for pride—pride that manifested itself in forsaking Jehovah and chasing after Baal. And when that happened, this text says, *he died.*

This clearly does not mean that the tribe itself ceased to exist. Mathew Henry says:

> "When Ephraim forsook God, and took to worship images, the state received its death's wound and was never good for any thing afterwards. Note, Deserting God is the death of any person or persons." (Henry, 1192)

We can see a similar thing in the United Kingdom of our day. It used to be a distinctly Christian nation, the home of people like Spurgeon and Bunyan, and a prolific sender of missionaries. But as it has become less and less a Christian nation, now even going so far as a police officer threatening people for singing church hymns in public, it has, in effect, already died. It is a shadow of its former self both in size and in influence and is growing weaker by the day. (Duell, 2024)

A choice to multiply sin

Hosea 13:2 *And now they sin more and more, and have made them molten images of their silver, and idols according to their own understanding, all of it the work of the craftsmen: they say of them, Let the men that sacrifice kiss the calves.*

Sin is never a thing that can be satisfied; it will always require more participation, more adoration, and more degradation. And all of that is seen in this verse. Once they started down the pathway of idolatry, they sinned more and more. They took their silver, blessings from God, and made images and idols from it, gods of "their own understanding." As with so many today, the revealed God was not palatable to them, so they made a god they could be comfortable with.

The last phrase of the verse, *Let the men that sacrifice kiss the calves,* is an interesting one. You see, this was a test of true adoration. In order to keep people from secretly believing in Jehovah and then just pretending to worship the idols when they came to offer sacrifice, they would require the sacrificers to openly kiss the idols.

Here is a famous reference to that:

1 Kings 19:18 *Yet I have left me seven thousand in Israel, all the knees which have not bowed unto Baal, and every mouth which hath not kissed him.*

So in Hosea's day, there were more and more idols, and everyone was expected to put their lips to the metal to prove their adoration of them.

A cost for a wicked path

Hosea 13:3 *Therefore they shall be as the morning cloud, and as the early dew that passeth away, as the chaff that is driven with the whirlwind out of the floor, and as the smoke out of the chimney.*

What would happen to idolatrous Israel? God used four pictures here to describe their one end. Both the morning cloud and the early dew evaporate away as the sun rises and begins to warm the land. The chaff, the fine dust from off of the grain, gets completely blown away when the strong wind races across the threshing floor. The smoke that rises out of the chimney floats away and dissipates.

All of this was being applied to Israel! This strong, proud nation was going to be reduced to helpless insignificance because of their chosen idolatrous path.

A command of absolute devotion

Hosea 13:4 *Yet I am the LORD thy God from the land of Egypt, and thou shalt know no god but me: for there is no saviour beside me.*

These were not at all new or unfamiliar words to Israel. In fact, as soon as God brought them out of Egypt, He immediately started telling them this—and had it set in stone:

Exodus 20:1 *And God spake all these words, saying,* **2** *I am the LORD thy God, which have brought thee out of the land of Egypt, out of the house of bondage.* **3** *Thou shalt have no other gods before me.*

He went on to repeat it throughout their history:

Isaiah 43:11 *I, even I, am the LORD; and beside me there is no saviour.*

Hosea 12:9 *And I that am the LORD thy God from the land of Egypt will yet make thee to dwell in tabernacles, as in the days of the solemn feast.*

This was not just a historical reminder; it was a continued command of absolute devotion to Jehovah alone. The end of the verse says, *and thou shalt know no god but me: for there is no saviour beside me.*

This was God's expectation that Israel would neither believe in nor even have any regard for any other god since He alone was their Savior. They knew of many gods in Egypt; none delivered them from bondage. They knew of many gods in Canaan; none kept them from one captivity after another. But the entire time they followed Jehovah, they were free; that all by itself should have been enough for them to be completely devoted to their God, the one true God.

A conundrum of forgetfulness

Hosea 13:5 *I did know thee in the wilderness, in the land of great drought.* **6** *According to their pasture, so were they filled; they were filled, and their heart was exalted; therefore have they forgotten me.*

There are many decades of history in these two verses. Verse five is referring back to their forty years in the wilderness;

God described that situation elsewhere in the same kind of terms He did here:

Deuteronomy 2:7 *For the LORD thy God hath blessed thee in all the works of thy hand: he knoweth thy walking through this great wilderness: these forty years the LORD thy God hath been with thee; thou hast lacked nothing.*

Deuteronomy 8:15 *Who led thee through that great and terrible wilderness, wherein were fiery serpents, and scorpions, and drought, where there was no water; who brought thee forth water out of the rock of flint;*

Deuteronomy 32:10 *He found him in a desert land, and in the waste howling wilderness; he led him about, he instructed him, he kept him as the apple of his eye.*

Notice that God said that He knew them in that terrible wilderness. *Knew* is from the word *yada,* and it is a term of tenderness and intimacy. God did not just know those wandering, recently freed slaves in the sense of knowing who they were; He lovingly claimed them as His own when others would have been embarrassed by them.

Verse six takes us beyond the wilderness wanderings and into the many years that followed in the Promised Land. And the contrast is stark and shocking:

"According to their pasture, so were they filled; they were filled, and their heart was exalted; therefore have they forgotten me."

When they had nothing and were wandering in the desert like vagabonds, God knew them, God claimed them, God provided for them, God loved them. But once they got into the Promised Land and settled down, and once they got successful, they forgot Him. God was not embarrassed by them when they had nothing, but they were embarrassed by Him once they had everything.

Yes, that is horrible. IS horrible; present tense. You see, we in our day often do the exact same thing. When we have nothing and need everything, we love the fact that we can seek after God and that He loves us and takes care of us. But once He has allowed us to become successful and in need of nothing, we seem to be embarrassed of the way we used to lean on Him and cry out to Him and even cry and weep over how good He was to us.

There is no more horrible forgetfulness than that.

A consuming adversary

Hosea 13:7 *Therefore I will be unto them as a lion: as a leopard by the way will I observe them:* **8** *I will meet them as a bear that is bereaved of her whelps, and will rend the caul of their heart, and there will I devour them like a lion: the wild beast shall tear them.*

The central picture of these verses is incredibly obvious: lion, leopard, bear, lion, wild beast.

God said *therefore,* because they chose to forget Him when they felt like they no longer needed Him, He would be to them as a lion. Not as a defending lion; a devouring lion. He said that He would also be as a leopard observing them by the way, and for the purpose of pouncing on them for their destruction. He said that He would meet them as a bear bereaved of her whelps; in other words, as a mama bear whose cubs had been taken. He would *rend the caul of their heart,* meaning He would rip through the membrane surrounding it and sink His claws all the way down into the heart. He said that the wild beast would tear them, meaning that when He Himself was done with them, jackal-like creatures would also dig into the carcass.

If you get the sense that God coming to meet you once you have decided you do not need Him anymore is a bad thing, you are correct. God as an ally is utterly comforting; God as an adversary is utterly terrifying.

A call for subjects

Hosea 13:9 *O Israel, thou hast destroyed thyself; but in me is thine help.*

A fairly consistent and common complaint people have when everything begins to go wrong in their wicked lives is that God is to blame. God takes direct aim at that thought in the first half of this verse, pointing out that Israel's destruction was self-inflicted. She was already beginning to suffer the consequences of her own actions and would ultimately find herself taken away by the Assyrians because of her own choices.

But God is so good that in the last half of the verse He reminded them that, by contrast, *but in me is thine help.*

Help was still available. Though the decision to send them into captivity was already made, there could yet be mercy within that situation, and God had already promised mercy for future generations of Israel.

Whatever horrible things you are experiencing due to your own foolish choices, please understand that it does not have to get as bad as it can be; some measure of mercy is still available if you will repent and turn to God in earnestness.

Hosea 13:10 *I will be thy king: where is any other that may save thee in all thy cities? and thy judges of whom thou saidst, Give me a king and princes?*

God was always supposed to be their king. Even when they had a human king sitting on the throne, God was still supposed to be their KING. And He offered that again to them now, reminding them that, if they looked in every corner and nook and cranny of all of their cities, they would find neither judge nor king nor prince among their people who could deliver them.

Hosea 13:11 *I gave thee a king in mine anger, and took him away in my wrath.*

Segueing off of the kingship spoken of in verse ten, God now takes them back in time to the beginning of their earthly monarchy. When they rejected God and demanded a human king, God gave them one, namely Saul of Benjamin. But He did so in anger, not in approval. And they were soon to find out that badgering God into giving you something is the easiest way to make a supposed blessing a drastic curse. The very same king that God gave in His anger, He later took away in His wrath. Within two years of the beginning of Saul's reign, God had already determined to rip the kingdom away from him and give it to David.

Saul went on to be a hollow king and ingloriously took his own life in battle before the Philistines could do it for him. This became a stain and a national embarrassment on the people who demanded a human king to follow.

A costly lingering

Hosea 13:12 *The iniquity of Ephraim is bound up; his sin is hid.*

Let me explain some terms to you, so you do not get the wrong idea and think that Ephraim is the one doing the binding and the hiding of his sin in this verse.

Bound up is from the word *tsarar*. It "means to be bound up in a bundle, like a thing you wish to take great care of." *Hid* is from *tsaphan,* meaning "carefully preserved, so as not to be lost." (KD p.159)

In the context of all that has been said and the coming judgment that has been promised, it is evident that God is the One doing the bundling and preserving of Ephraim's sins. He is the One that is treasuring up all of this, not for the purpose of reward, but for the purpose of retribution.

Hosea 13:13 *The sorrows of a travailing woman shall come upon him: he is an unwise son; for he should not stay long in the place of the breaking forth of children.*

When you see the text say that the sorrows of a travailing woman shall come upon **him**, and that **he** is an unwise **son,** you understand quickly that this is a person experiencing something they did not need to experience. A him/he/son is not supposed to experience the sorrows of a woman going into labor; that is something that belongs to a woman, not to him.

The fact that Ephraim was going to experience all of the troubles that did not belong to him marked him as "an unwise son." And the concluding explanation of that at the end of the verse is *for he should not stay long in the place of the breaking forth of children.*

This description changes the picture just a bit. In these words, Ephraim becomes the baby being birthed, a baby that somehow chooses to just hang out in the birthing canal and not be brought into the world.

A baby that does that will die, every single time.

The picture here is that God wanted to bring Israel/Ephraim to new life, namely a life of walking only with Him, but they chose to linger in their old life of idolatry and die instead.

A coming deliverance

Hosea 13:14 *I will ransom them from the power of the grave; I will redeem them from death: O death, I will be thy plagues; O grave, I will be thy destruction: repentance shall be hid from mine eyes.*

Verse fourteen is a bit of a prophetical whiplash. Verse thirteen gave the picture of Ephraim in his foolishness dying in the womb of idolatry. Verses fifteen and sixteen will use graphic terminology to describe the horrible devastation she is about to experience. But right in the middle of those two points, verse fourteen gives God's promise that He will ransom His people from the power of the grave and redeem them from death.

This was a light piercing the most suffocating darkness, a promise that though the near future was going to be bleak, the distant future was going to be blessed.

The picture given at the end of the verse is powerful:

O death, I will be thy plagues; O grave, I will be thy destruction: repentance shall be hid from mine eyes.

The death and grave He is talking about is Assyria, the people who would become death and the grave to His people, Israel. God was going to be the plague and the destruction to Assyria. And He was so set on this that He said, *repentance shall be hid from mine eyes*, meaning that He would not even listen when Assyria cried out for mercy and repented of what they had done to Israel.

Israel would be reborn, and neither Assyria nor Babylon nor all the demons and devils of Hell could ever stop it.

A consuming wind

Hosea 13:15 *Though he be fruitful among his brethren, an east wind shall come, the wind of the LORD shall come up from the wilderness, and his spring shall become dry, and his fountain shall be dried up: he shall spoil the treasure of all pleasant vessels.*

From the delight of verse fourteen, the scene now shifts back to the devastation here in verse fifteen. The *he* of verse fifteen is Ephraim. In fact, there is even a play on his name in this verse. The word fruitful is pointing back to the fact that the name Ephraim means doubly fruitful. Joseph named his son Ephraim because he intended for him to be fruitful. And in the present moment of Hosea's day, Ephraim/Israel was indeed fruitful. Again, it was a time of great prosperity. But in spite of this, God said that *an east wind shall come, the wind of the LORD shall come up from the wilderness.*

Assyria was that east wind that God was going to send as judgment against His people. And the first stated result of that was going to be that *his spring shall become dry, and his fountain shall be dried up.* A land without a water source in those days was doomed; God was going to cut off everything that could have given them life.

The second stated result of this was that *he* [the invading Assyrian army] *shall spoil the treasure of all pleasant vessels.* Whatever Israel had that was worth taking, Assyria was going to take it.

Hosea 13:16 *Samaria shall become desolate; for she hath rebelled against her God: they shall fall by the sword: their infants shall be dashed in pieces, and their women with child shall be ripped up.*

Samaria, the capital of the Northern Kingdom of Israel, was going to become desolate because of her rebellion against God. And the worst part of all of that was going to be what happened to those among them who were the most vulnerable. Yes, the soldiers would *fall by the sword,* but that is to be expected in battle. The heart-wrenching part is what follows: *their infants shall be dashed in pieces, and their women with child shall be ripped up.*

Infants, pregnant young women, and even babies in the womb were going to become victims of the savagery of the invading Assyrian army. Israel turned to devils, and those devils would now turn on Israel and do what devils do.

I took a picture many years ago, and to this day it is one of my favorite pictures. I was coming home from a meeting in

Tennessee, driving down an obscure country road, and I happened to look up on the trunk of a pine tree by the side of the road and see an old metal sign:

Welcome To Struggleville, U.S.A.

I turned the car around, and I went back and took a picture of that sign. I do not know who put it up or how long it has been there or what trials and tribulations prompted someone to make and post it.

I do know that the quickest way to get to Struggleville is by the pride that leads a person or a nation to reject the authority of God in their lives.

Chapter Seventeen
I Will Love Them Freely

Hosea 14:1 *O Israel, return unto the LORD thy God; for thou hast fallen by thine iniquity.* **2** *Take with you words, and turn to the LORD: say unto him, Take away all iniquity, and receive us graciously: so will we render the calves of our lips.* **3** *Asshur shall not save us; we will not ride upon horses: neither will we say any more to the work of our hands, Ye are our gods: for in thee the fatherless findeth mercy.* **4** *I will heal their backsliding, I will love them freely: for mine anger is turned away from him.* **5** *I will be as the dew unto Israel: he shall grow as the lily, and cast forth his roots as Lebanon.* **6** *His branches shall spread, and his beauty shall be as the olive tree, and his smell as Lebanon.* **7** *They that dwell under his shadow shall return; they shall revive as the corn, and grow as the vine: the scent thereof shall be as the wine of Lebanon.* **8** *Ephraim shall say, What have I to do any more with idols? I have heard him, and observed him: I am like a green fir tree. From me is thy fruit found.* **9** *Who is wise, and he shall understand these things? prudent, and he shall know them? for the ways of the LORD are right, and the just shall walk in them: but the transgressors shall fall therein.*

In case you have forgotten the real life drama that became the living illustration of the main content of the book of Hosea, Hosea the prophet married a woman that no one would have expected him to have anything to do with. At the express command of God, he married a woman of ill repute; he took her in and loved her when everyone would have expected a man of his stature to have nothing but loathing for her.

And yet in spite of that, she cheated on him and broke the marriage. She left him and the children in order to pursue her old life of sin. At that point, he had every right to divorce her. In fact, under the law of Moses, he had every right to have her stoned. But instead, he chose what I call *The Hosea Option*. He chose to love her enough to do whatever was necessary to break her from her wickedness. And once she was broken, broken and used up and scarred and unwanted by any other, he expressed the most magnificent love imaginable; he bought her back from the slave market. But not as a slave, mind you, not as one to torment with her self-induced weakness and his position of power; he bought her back to once again love her with all his heart.

And then Hosea and Gomer faded from the text, left to their lives together. For the past ten chapters, everything has been about Israel who behaved like Gomer, and God who behaved like Hosea. And all of that will now culminate in this inexpressibly beautiful chapter.

A merciful call

Hosea 14:1 *O Israel, return unto the LORD thy God; for thou hast fallen by thine iniquity.*

In the relationship between Hosea and Gomer, the problem never was that Hosea left Gomer; the problem was always that Gomer left Hosea. Likewise, in the relationship between God and Israel, the problem was never that God left Israel; the problem was always that Israel left God. And since it was Israel that forsook the LORD, it was Israel that must return unto the LORD.

And that is exactly what God through Hosea called out to Israel in this verse. They had both the opportunity and the command to return to the LORD. God had no desire for them to stay estranged; the express desire of His heart was for them to be restored. Yes, they were going to go into captivity. Yes, they were going to lose their land and their monarchy. But far more important than their land and monarchy was their relationship with the God, Who gave them birth as a nation. And that could be restored whether in Israel or in Assyria.

At the end of verse one, He gave them a quick reminder of why and how it had come to this point, saying, *for thou hast fallen by thine iniquity.*

As they were reading those words, though they had fallen spiritually, they had not yet fallen nationally; yet God expressed what was going to happen in terms as certain as if it had already happened since there was no question that it was going to happen. Their iniquity had turned a free people into a fallen people; iniquity always eventually breaks and enslaves the one who pursues it.

Hosea 14:2 *Take with you words, and turn to the LORD: say unto him, Take away all iniquity, and receive us graciously: so will we render the calves of our lips.*

As we begin to examine verse two, one thing you should know is that the word turn is from the exact same word as return in verse one. Both are from the word *shoob,* and both mean to turn back, or in theological terms, to repent.

So Israel was commanded to repent; they were commanded to turn back to the LORD. But as we begin to look at verse two, we find that the initial command in this is *take with you words, and turn to the Lord.* There were, therefore, some things that God was going to expect to hear from them if they were truly repentant. A person who has truly turned back to the Lord will speak differently from a person who is still ensconced in their sin.

But what exactly was it that God was expecting to hear? The verse lays it out for us distinctly: *say unto him, Take away all iniquity, and receive us graciously: so will we render the calves of our lips.*

God was first of all expecting to hear them ask Him to take away all of their iniquity. And please understand that they were to be asking for their actual iniquity to be removed, not merely the penalty for their iniquity. Lots of people ask God to remove the *consequences* of their fornication or their adultery or their drunkenness or their lying or their unfaithfulness, but far fewer ask God to remove the sin itself. Far fewer are praying, "God, no matter what you have to do to me, do not ever let me commit fornication or adultery again, do not ever let me touch another drop of alcohol, do not ever let me be unfaithful," and you can fill in the blank with any other sin ever committed by man.

The one who is truly repentant wants God to remove the sin from their life, not just the consequences of that sin.

The second thing God was expecting to hear, though, was *And receive us graciously*. In these words, we find the proper heart attitude that accompanies repentance, an attitude of realization that we cannot come on our own merit but must be received and restored as an act of God's grace alone. In general, people think far too highly of themselves for God to actually be willing to receive them.

The last phrase of the verse, *so will we render the calves of our lips*, was designed to bring to mind the sacrificial system of worship Israel was to employ. When they came to worship the Lord, they did not come empty-handed; they brought something such as a calf to give to Him as a sacrifice. But in this case, it was not the calves of the field but the calves of human lips that God was expecting to be brought. And that very clearly ties into everything that has come before in this verse; God was expecting to hear the right things from them, humble and repentant words from a contrite heart.

Hosea 14:3 *Asshur shall not save us; we will not ride upon horses: neither will we say any more to the work of our hands, Ye are our gods: for in thee the fatherless findeth mercy.*

Verse three continues the list of expectations that God had for what was to be coming out of the mouths of His repentant people. And there were two particular sins they were to be verbally and from the heart repenting of in this verse. They were first of all to be saying, *Asshur shall not save us; we will not ride upon horses*.

This is the first time the word Asshur has appeared in the book of Hosea in English. But you have seen it in another word repeatedly; it is the same word for Assyria. And when you compare this verse to a couple of earlier verses in the book of Hosea, it is not at all difficult to understand what these words mean:

Hosea 5:13 *When Ephraim saw his sickness, and Judah saw his wound, then went Ephraim to the Assyrian, and sent to king Jareb: yet could he not heal you, nor cure you of your wound.*

Hosea 7:11 *Ephraim also is like a silly dove without heart: they call to Egypt, they go to Assyria.*

Israel repeatedly bounced back and forth between seeking help from forging alliances with Assyria (Ashur) and Egypt with their famed horses and chariots. So the repentant words that God is expecting them to say were to be a reflection that they would no longer seek their help from those who were by nature their enemies! From now on, they would always and only seek their help from the God who loved them so dearly.

The second thing He was expecting from their repentant lips was not something that they would say, but something that they would never again say: *neither will we say any more to the work of our hands, Ye are our gods.*

This is not at all difficult to understand. God was expecting His repentant people to never again look at dumb, lifeless pieces of wood that they had carved and plated with metal and say, "You are our gods!"

From their perspective, though, people who had been engaged in this very wickedness for so long that it was all the living had ever known, why would they be willing to repent in such manner? The answer is given at the end of the verse, *for in thee the fatherless findeth mercy.*

For all practical purposes, Israel was a fatherless people. Mind you, it was entirely their doing; they were the ones who pushed their heavenly Father away. But their God was and is a God in which the fatherless can still find mercy.

And both in their coming captivity and in their eventual restoration, they were going to need it.

A majestic love

Hosea 14:4 *I will heal their backsliding, I will love them freely: for mine anger is turned away from him.*

After all of the scathing and scalding promises of the coming judgment, these had to be the most beautiful words Israel ever heard from God through the lips of Hosea. From here to the end of the book, save for one small warning in the very last verse, the book of Hosea closes with everything being well, with Israel returning to God and with God restoring them just as fully and more so than Hosea restored Gomer.

God made three promises in this verse. Promise number one was *I will heal their backsliding.* And this was not just the wishful thinking of Hosea, who loved his people; God said the exact same thing to His people through Jeremiah the prophet as well:

Jeremiah 3:22 *Return, ye backsliding children, and <u>I will heal your backslidings</u>. Behold, we come unto thee; for thou art the LORD our God.*

In both cases, the word God used for healing was the word *Rapha,* which is part of the compound name of God Jehovah Rapha, meaning the God who heals. And the fact that it was backsliding that He was going to heal them of paints backsliding itself as a loathsome, putrid disease of the human spirit.

God loved them too much to leave them that way, so He determined to heal them of that backsliding.

The second promise He made was *I will love them freely.* Freely is from the word *nadabah*, and it means gratuitous, liberal, and unmerited. In our terms, God's promise to love them freely means the same thing as lavishly. This was not going to be some measured, gradual, tempered love from the God who was still stewing over the behavior of His people; this was going to be a love that chose to forget the past and treat Israel as if all had always been well.

The third promise was, *for mine anger is turned away from him*. Just as the people would turn away from their sin and back to their God, God was going to turn His anger away from the people. From then on, when they looked to their God, they would no longer see as it were anger on His face; it simply would not be there.

Hosea 14:5 *I will be as the dew unto Israel: he shall grow as the lily, and cast forth his roots as Lebanon.*

The metaphors God uses in this verse are exquisite. The first is *I will be as the dew unto Israel*. There in the parched and dry Middle East, God promised His fading people that He would be like the dew unto them. He would be their refreshment, He would be their source of life. The second is *he shall grow as the lily*. God has referred to His people by many agricultural terms in this book, but this is the first time He has spoken of the lily.

He was going to take people who were little more than spiritual weeds by that point and turn them into the most beautiful flowers. The third is *and cast forth his roots as Lebanon*. The trees of Lebanon were famed the world over for having roots that went down nearly as far as their height into the air. God was going to take people who were shallow and easily movable and plant them with roots so deep that they could practically no longer be moved.

Hosea 14:6 *His branches shall spread, and his beauty shall be as the olive tree, and his smell as Lebanon.*

Continuing with the metaphor of a tree, God promised that Israel's branches would spread and that his beauty would be as the olive tree and that his smell would be like the trees of Lebanon, most of which were fragrant cedars.

Hosea 14:7 *They that dwell under his shadow shall return; they shall revive as the corn, and grow as the vine: the scent thereof shall be as the wine of Lebanon.*

Still picturing Israel as a tree, God spoke of the day to come when the people of Israel would come and dwell under the shadow of his, the nation of Israel's branches. This was no less a national rebirth and restoration.

The people that came home would also be revived as the corn. And I love Adam Clarke's description of this:

> "The justness and beauty of this metaphor is not generally perceived. After the corn has been a short time above the earth, in a single spike, the blades begin to separate, and the stalk to spring out of the centre. The side leaves turn back to make way for the protruding stalk; and fall bending down to the earth, assuming a withered appearance, though still attached to the plant. To look at the corn in this state, no one, unacquainted with the circumstance, could entertain any sanguine hope of a copious harvest.

In a short time other leaves spring out; the former freshen, and begin to stand erect; and the whole seems to revive from a vegetative death." (Clarke, 654)

Just like that, Israel, who looked for all appearances to be dead, would be revived to vibrant new life.

They would also *grow as the vine*. We have at our home both grapevines and muscadine vines. And we see the same thing that tenders of vines the world over have always seen. During the wintertime, to look at that vine you would be absolutely convinced that it is utterly dead. But in the springtime, it blooms out to new life, and all the seeming deadness of the winter is forgotten. This is what Israel was going to be like when God revived her.

God also promised that *the scent thereof shall be as the wine of Lebanon*. The wines of Lebanon were famed for their lovely and aromatic scent. God was going to take His putrid, rotten-smelling people and make them a sweet savor in His nostrils once again.

A marvelous conclusion

Hosea 14:8 *Ephraim shall say, What have I to do any more with idols? I have heard him, and observed him: I am like a green fir tree. From me is thy fruit found.*

To understand verse eight, you need to know that there are two voices in it. The first voice is obviously that of Ephraim. And his words go to the colon in the sentence. So Ephraim/Israel has the first half of the verse, saying, *What have I to do any more with idols? I have heard him, and observed him.* And the *him* that Ephraim has observed is the God that has been trying to get his attention the whole time. Thus, Ephraim's words here mean, "Why in the world would I want idols anymore? I have finally heard and seen the real God!" And God, hearing that proclamation from the heart of Ephraim, responds with the words, *I am like a green fir tree. From me is thy fruit found.* In so many words, He was saying, "That's good, Ephraim, very good. You have tried your dead, dry hunks of wood that you made idols out of, and they have done nothing to sustain you. I am different; I am like the majestic green fir tree; I am alive. And while your idols could never sustain you, you will always find fruit for your sustenance in me."

Hosea 14:9 *Who is wise, and he shall understand these things? prudent, and he shall know them? for the ways of the LORD are right, and the just shall walk in them: but the transgressors shall fall therein.*

Hosea 14:9 is the epilogue to the book. It is what comes after the "The End" of the story. This is God asking some questions of all of us based on what He has written to us and for us in the book Hosea. He first of all wants to know *Who is wise, and he shall understand these things? prudent, and he shall know them?* In other words, "Who gets it? I have written this entire account to you, both the biographical account of Hosea and Gomer and the theological account of God and Israel, and I have done that so that you can learn the lessons from it that you should. So, who gets it?

And then He concludes with, *for the ways of the LORD are right, and the just shall walk in them: but the transgressors shall fall therein.* All through the book of Hosea, this choice has been laid out. Whether our flesh ever likes them or not, the ways of the Lord are right; they are always right. And the just, the truly righteous, will walk in those ways. By contrast, the transgressors shall fall therein.

That last phrase is amazing, really. We would expect the transgressors to fall out of the ways of the Lord, but here we find them falling in the ways of the Lord. In other words, they would still be performing all of their outward religious ceremonies and duties, but their hearts would be so corrupt that they would fall headlong into iniquity anyway.

Just being religious will never be enough; there absolutely must be repentance that leads to a relationship that leads to real righteousness if we are going to stand in the ways of the Lord rather than fall in the ways of the Lord.

But the fact that that is even an option by the end of this book is absolutely amazing. After all Israel did to push God away, after all the ways they repeatedly broke His heart, when everything was said and done, God had brought things right back around to "I will love them freely." They were broken, they were dirty, they were used up... and God still determined to love them freely and to restore them to real righteousness.

That really is *Love When It Matters Most.*

Works Cited

Ahlheim, B. (2016, September 9). *Superstar megachurch son of a (hopefully ashamed) preacher man Andy Stanley: Scripture can't be defended.* Pulpit & Pen News. https://pulpitandpen.org/2016/08/30/superstar-mega-church-son-of-a-hopefully-ashamed-preacher-man-andy-stanley-scripture-cant-be-defended/

Ayers, E. (2024d, September 16). *Pope Francis draws criticism for saying all religions are a path to god.* The Washington Times. https://www.washingtontimes.com/news/2024/sep/16/pope-francis-draws-criticism-for-saying-all-religi/

Clarke, Adam. *The Holy Bible, Containing the Old and New Testaments, the Text Carefully Printed from the Most Correct Copies of the Present Authorized Translation, Including the Marginal Readings and Parallel Texts: with a Commentary and Critical Notes Designed as a Help to a Better Understanding of the Sacred Writings.* Vol. 4, Abingdon, 1977.

Duell, M. (2024, January 29). *Moment volunteer police officer tells Christian singer on Oxford Street that she is "not allowed" to perform "church songs outside of Church Grounds" before walking off and sticking her tongue out to the camera.* Daily Mail Online. https://www.dailymail.co.uk/news/article-13018183/police-officer-christian-singer-oxford-street-church-songs-outside.html

Feinberg, C. L. (1952). *The Minor Prophets.* Moody Press.

Henry, Matthew. *Matthew Henrys' Commentary of the Whole Bible.* Vol. 4, Fleming H Revell

ISBE, <u>International Standard Bible Encyclopaedia.</u> Vol. 4, Grand Rapids: Eerdmans, MI, 1955.

Jamieson, R., Fausset, A. R., & Brown, D.. *A commentary on the old and new testaments.* Vol. 2, 2008

Keil, C. F., & Delitzsch, F. J. (1950). *Biblical Commentary on The Old Testament: The Twelve Minor Prophets* (J. Martin, Trans.; Vol. 1). Eerdmans.

Linder, Phil. Power Bible CD v 5.9, 2010

Woke pastor rewrites jesus' parables in worse possible way: "the kingdom of god is like the trans woman athlete..." Protestia. (2024, September 18). https://protestia.com/2024/09/18/woke-pastor-rewrites-jesus-parables-in-worse-possible-way-the-kingdom-of-god-is-like-trans-woman-athlete/

Other Books by Pastor Bo Wagner

Colossians: The Treasures of Deity
Daniel: Breathtaking
Ephesians: The Treasures of Family
Esther: Five Feasts and the Fingerprints of God
Galatians: Treasures of Liberty
James: The Pen and the Plumb Line
Jonah: A Story of Greatness
Nehemiah: A Labor of Love
Philippians: The Treasures of Joy
Proverbs Vol 1: Bright Light from Dark Sayings
Proverbs Vol 2: Bright Light from Dark Sayings
The Revelation: Ready or Not
Romans: Salvation from A-Z
Ruth: Diamonds in the Darkness

Beyond the Colored Coat
From Footers to Finish Nails
Learning Not to Fear the Old Testament
Marriage Makers/Marriage Breakers
I'm Saved! Now What???
Don't Muzzle the Ox
Why Christmas?

Books in the Night Heroes Series

Cry from the Coal Mine (Vol 1)
Free Fall (Vol 2)
Broken Brotherhood (Vol 3)
The Blade of Black Crow (Vol 4)
Ghost Ship (Vol 5)
When Serpents Rise (Vol 6)

Moth Man (Vol 7)
Runaway (Vol 8)
Terror by Day (Vol 9)
Winter Wolf (Vol 10)
Desert Heat (Vol 11)
Deadline (Vol 12)
The Sword and the Iron Curtain (Vol 13)

Other Fiction

Zak Blue: Falcon Wing
Zak Blue: Enter the Maelstrom

Devotionals

DO Drops Vol. 1
DO Drops Vol. 2
DO Drops Vol. 3
DO Drops Vol. 4
DO Drops Vol. 5
DO Drops Vol. 6
DO Drops Vol. 7
DO Drops Vol. 8
DO Drops Vol. 9
DO Drops Vol 10
DO Drops Vol 11
DO Drops Vol 12

www.ingramcontent.com/pod-product-compliance
Lightning Source LLC
Chambersburg PA
CBHW071311110426
42743CB00042B/1266